ADVICE
from the
RUDD
CLINIC

A Guide
to Colorectal Health

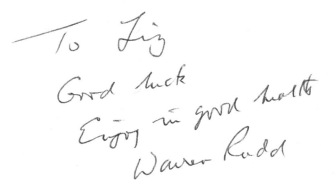

To Liz
Good luck
Enjoy in good health
Warren Rudd

To ensure good colorectal health, you should know:

- You can't get hemorrhoids from sitting on a cold surface.

- You *can* get hemorrhoids if you sit on the toilet for a long time—try to find somewhere else to read!

- Hemorrhoids and piles are the same thing. They're not painful and they can now all be treated by a simple office procedure.

- The painful anal swelling sometimes experienced by pregnant women is *not* caused by hemorrhoids. This is usually the sign of a hematoma which will heal within a month and may not recur.

- The most frequently missed anal diagnosis is anusitis—an anal irritation that can be treated with Anurex, a reusable cold suppository or simply by changing the diet.

- There are two kinds of fibre—soluble and insoluble. Only one helps constipation. How much insoluble fibre do you need?

- Eating the right kind of fibre will only help if you drink water with it.

- 1 in 20 Canadians will get colon cancer—men and women in almost equal numbers.

- All colon cancers originate within benign polyps and almost all polyps in the colon can be removed before they become cancerous. Colon cancer is one of the only major cancers that may be stopped before it has a chance to start.

ADVICE

from the

RUDD
CLINIC

A Guide to Colorectal Health

Wm Warren Rudd, M.D.

Colon & Rectal Surgeon
Founder and Director of The Rudd Clinic
for Diseases of the Colon and Rectum
Toronto

Canadian Cataloguing in Publication Data

Rudd, Wm Warren (William Warren)
Advice from the Rudd clinic : a guide to colorectal health

Includes index.

ISBN 0-9685711-0-7

1. Colon (Anatomy) – Diseases.   2. Rectum – Diseases.
I. Title.

RC860.R83 1997   616.3'4   C97-930324-9

2 3 4 5 B–G 01 00 99
Second printing July 1999
Illustrations by Theresa Sakno, B.Sc. BMC
Text design by Gord Robertson
Author photo by Portraits by Mina

Printed in Canada

Contents

Foreword

WARREN BUFFET, one of the world's smartest investors, says that Rule No. 1 in finance is never to lose capital. And Rule No. 2 is never, never forget Rule No. 1. Today, in medicine, Rule No. 1 for a long and healthy life is to practice prevention. And Rule No. 2 is never, never forget Rule No. 1.

Prevention is the primary theme of Dr. Rudd's book. Many of the conditions he discusses in his fluent and practical style do not have to happen.

One of Harvard's esteemed professors of surgery once passed along succinct advice. He told his medical class that "if you fail to put your finger in the rectum you often end up putting your foot in it" by failing to diagnose a rectal cancer!

Dr. Rudd has always gone a step farther. For years, he has emphasized that rectal examination alone is not enough to rule out malignancy. Rather, his "gold standard" is colonoscopic examination. This procedure explores the entire colon to find premalignant polyps.

For years we have been able to eliminate needless cancers of the cervix in women. But this can't be done without annual Pap smears. Now another malignancy, cancer of the large bowel and rectum, can be almost wiped out. But only if, as Dr. Rudd stresses, both sexes are willing to have colonoscopic examinations every 5 years. Consider the frightening alternative to colonoscopy. If a cancer of the large bowel is discovered as soon as symptoms occur, it's usually an advanced malignancy. The 15-year survival rate is 20%. But if a cancer is detected before symptoms occur, the survival rate jumps to 80%.

Why not shoot for 100% survival? It can be achieved when a premalignant polyp is discovered and removed during a regular colonoscopic examination. This is what preventive medicine is all about. And it's what Dr. Rudd has been preaching for years. Audrey Hepburn would, in all probability, be alive today if she had had the chance to read Dr. Rudd's book and act on his advice.

How many of us will listen? André Gide, the distinguished French novelist, once began a lecture by saying, "Everything has been said before, but since nobody listened we have to keep going back and begin all over again." Prevention, reasonable as it seems, is always a tough sell. But the wise medical consumer listens to this message and takes immediate action.

Dr. Rudd conveys another vital message throughout his book. It's that lifestyle is often the key to a long and healthy life.

I'm sure all of us are happy to be living in North America. We enjoy many of the benefits of living in the developed world. Unfortunately, not enough of us realize we also suffer from medical problems associated with industrialized nations.

Compared, for instance, with Ugandans, millions of North Americans have crippled their bowels. The people of Uganda eat huge amounts of fibre. Canadians and Americans, on the other hand, lack sufficient fibre in their diets.

On the surface this appears to be a small, insignificant difference. But that's not the case. It can mean the pain and discomfort of diverticulitis, or the inconvenience of hemorrhoids, or even the difference between life and death.

The people of Uganda rarely develop cancers of the colon and rectum. Dr. Rudd explains that this is largely due to their fibre intake.

Dr. Rudd's book is of particular value at a time when our health-care system is suffering from severe financial problems. In both Canada and the U.S., measures are being instituted to decrease the escalating costs of medical care.

This book offers one prime way to do it. Many of the procedures discussed in the book can be performed effectively and without pain in a doctor's office, rather than in an expensive hospital setting.

Not everyone suffers a heart attack, diabetes, a broken leg or a variety of other diseases. But few, if any, people, will go through life without suffering from one or more of the conditions covered in this book. Equally important, it's written by a surgeon of outstanding authority who continues to be ahead of his time.

Reading this book will be time well spent. It has been aptly said that if we do not take the time to prevent disease, we will have to take the time for illness!

Dr. Ken Walker

Preface

I N MORE than 25 years of practice, during which I have seen tens of thousands of patients, I have been asked many questions about colon and rectal problems. After hearing the same questions so often and realizing there are no books available that cover this field, I had the idea of putting the answers to these questions in a book. For most of these questions, the answers are simple, but some of the misconceptions and myths are very hard to dispel. I have always endeavoured to make our techniques at the Rudd Clinic simple and more effective. Similarly, I hope all the practice I've had answering questions has helped me make the explanations in this book simple and easy to understand.

Throughout the book is advice that, I hope, will allow people to understand, diagnose and treat some of their own and their family's problems and also learn when to seek help from their doctor or specialist. Reading and learning about the problem could help relieve worry and avoid unnecessary trips to the hospital, not to mention avoid outdated procedures and possible complications. Health care is changing rapidly: new techniques are constantly being developed that make some of the common practices obsolete.

Possibly my most worthwhile contributions to my specialty and the main reasons for writing this book are to introduce to the public for the first time the topics of anusitis and anal stenosis, the two most frequently missed anal diagnoses, and to promote the prevention of colon cancer. Most of the procedures covered in this book can be done in the doctor's office, at huge savings to government and insurers. For example, using the new office treatment for hemorrhoids at the Rudd Clinic in Toronto has saved government more than $150 million. This figure increases dramatically when the savings using all the other office procedures done at the Rudd Clinic and by other doctors who have adopted them in their own practice are added up. Aside from the cost, these procedures are done much more quickly and efficiently, usually with less pain and with equal or better results, all without the added stress of hospital surgery. Not all doctors will agree with some of my recommendations.

I like to teach and have done so all over North America, in Europe and in Asia, but usually only to doctors. I would like to reach out to help everyone else. After all, it's the person suffering from the problem who is likely to get the most from this book. And once you understand what's involved, how to talk about a part of your body that isn't usually talked about and what to expect at the doctor's office, you're more likely to deal with health problems before they get serious.

It always amazes me how many people refuse to go to the doctor because they are afraid of what they might find. Most people believe in preventive maintenance for their car, but don't practice it for their bodies. Colon cancer is a perfect example of a potentially fatal disease that can usually be prevented by routine check-ups. This is one of the most important messages in this book; it is also one that is little known.

Ideally, this book should be read from cover to cover. The well-informed reader can then use the information to achieve optimal health as well as give good advice to family and friends, referring to the book again for specifics. But since each chapter is more or less self-contained, the section of most interest may be read separately.

To make this book as useful as possible and to fill a void in the literature, I've covered the most frequent problems encountered in my practice as a colorectal surgeon. The book is not meant to be an exhaustive encyclopedia. Since it covers only conditions that are frequently encountered, if you wish more information on less frequent diseases, please ask your doctor, check the library or bookstore, or contact the appropriate society (such as the Crohn's and Colitis Foundation of Canada).

Wm Warren Rudd, M.D.

With Thanks

I DEDICATE this book to my beautiful wife, Susan, who has always been a great support to me and deserves special thanks for her understanding and patience, and to our son, Bryce, who brings much laughter, insight and delight into our lives and is destined for great things.

I wish to thank Carla Caporiccio for all her help and patience over the years and for making my task much easier.

I am very grateful to Dr. Ken Walker for his continued support and encouragement, and to Peter Newman for being the catalyst to get this book published—without his stimulus this book might never have gotten off the ground.

My thanks, too, to my colleagues and staff at the Rudd Clinic for their ideas and comments, and to my editor, Madeline Koch, for her expertise and clear vision, and for keeping me out of trouble and in good humour.

I would also like to thank my patients, who have given me all this experience, without which I would never have learned and fine-tuned the techniques and advice that, I hope, have helped all the people treated at the Rudd Clinic in Toronto. May this book help many more.

1

Introduction

BEFORE COVERING such important topics as *what to do for itchiness* or *how to prevent colon cancer* or *the two most frequently missed anal diagnoses—anal stenosis* and *anusitis*—let's first go over some of the medical terms involved in this area of health care. In this chapter I also briefly explain how food progresses from top to bottom and what happens to *stool*, the part that isn't used for nutrition. Since knowing what to expect at the doctor's office, especially what kinds of examinations are used, can make all the difference, in "At the Doctor's Office" I discuss what preparation is required and what positions are used for anal examinations—and tackle the subject of HIV and AIDS and how doctors reduce the risk of spreading the virus. Being well informed and well prepared is a good way to stay healthy.

Anatomy and Function

The anatomy of the digestive tract is quite simple. If we follow the path of food after it is swallowed, we see that it goes down the *esophagus* and enters the *stomach*, where it is mixed with the gastric juices and enzymes, churned up and partly broken down. Then it goes into the *small bowel*, which is about 20 feet (6 m) long, where digestion continues. The small bowel empties into the *cecum* and travels along to the *colon*, where what is left of the food—the stool—ends up in the *rectum*. In order for the rectum to empty, the stool must pass out through the *anal canal*. This canal, only 1¼ inches (3 cm) long, is surrounded by the *sphincter muscles*, which control when the rectum can be emptied.

  The anal canal is divided into two parts by the *dentate line* (see Figure 1). The part above the dentate line has no pain nerves. The part below the line is lined by skin, which has pain nerves, just like skin everywhere else. That's why blood clots and fissures, which occur below the dentate line, are painful and why piles, which occur above the line, are usually not. In fact, that is why treatment for piles (hemorrhoids) need not hurt, because an operation above the dentate line is almost painless. The new treatment for piles takes advantage of this.

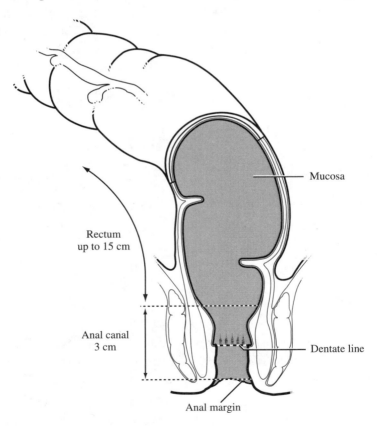

Figure 1: Anal Canal and part of rectum

There are a number of *glands* all around the anal canal just above the dentate line. Surrounding the canal are the sphincter muscles, which consist of two parts (see Figure 2). The *internal sphincter* is normally always tight and prevents gas from escaping on its own. The *external sphincter* can be tightened at will to keep stool back in the rectum and prevent accidents—a very important muscle. However, it tires easily and can only hold back for short periods. The sphincter contains a very sophisticated and detailed nerve supply that can even detect the difference between gas and liquid stool.

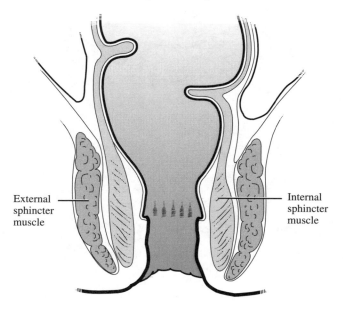

External
sphincter
muscle

Internal
sphincter
muscle

Figure 2: Sphincter Muscles

The colon, about 5 feet (125 cm) long, is also called the *large bowel* because it is three times the diameter of the small bowel. It is divided into five areas: the *cecum, ascending, transverse, descending* and *sigmoid* colon (see Figure 3). Since almost all polyps and cancers occur in the colon and rectum, we will concentrate on it, along with the rectum and the anal canal.

The food we eat is built of many simple particles or elements held together by bonds. These bonds are broken down by the enzymes

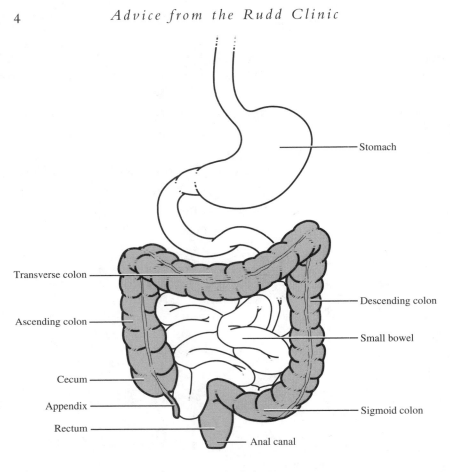

Figure 3: Colon

and juices in the small bowel. It is only in these simple elements that nutrients from the food can actually pass through the wall of the bowel and be absorbed into the bloodstream, to supply the body with nutrition. The food normally takes between 1 and 3 hours to pass from the mouth to the end of the small bowel. The remaining unabsorbed food is in a liquid form and empties into the colon, whose major function is water absorption. The stool starts out in the first part of the colon (cecum) and progresses along the ascending colon into the transverse, then the descending and sigmoid parts of the colon. All along this route, water passes out through the wall and into the bloodstream. The stool becomes more solid as it goes along, ending up in the rectum, where it is stored, held back by the sphincter muscles, until the rectum is full enough to signal that it needs to be emptied. The stool can be held back for a reasonable period until the appropriate time and place for a bowel movement.

It normally takes from 1 to 3 days for food to get through the colon. The speed at which food passes through anyone can be determined by a *transit study*—the person swallows a capsule containing little pellets and an x-ray is taken every 2 days, to observe how fast they travel through the bowel. If the stool passes through the colon too quickly, less water is absorbed, which results in loose, watery bowel movements—i.e., *diarrhea*. If the stool passes through too slowly, more water than normal is absorbed, which results in dry, hard stools—i.e., *constipation*.

At the Doctor's Office

Getting Ready to Go to the Doctor

Most people are embarrassed to talk to others about their bowel movements and anal opening. What makes this worse is when people hesitate because they are not sure of the right words to describe the area or the problem. This is slowly changing, however. Ten years ago, there was little talk about bowel habits (or sex, for that matter) in the open or in the media. There was little interest then in reading about this subject. Now the bookstores are full of medical self-help books (although I've yet to see one on colorectal health!). Times have changed.

Nevertheless, this is unfamiliar territory, and most of us are shy about entering it. But, for your own sake, make the effort to talk to your family doctor. This book should make it much easier: the familiarity with the area you gain here will decrease some of the embarrassment of the first visit (always the worst). Knowing what to expect should make it much easier for both you and your doctor. Even what you wear can help. Most doctors do not ask you to take off your clothes—only to lift up a skirt or pull down a pair of pants—and then cover you completely with a disposable sheet. You should wear loose-fitting clothes that will not crease—no bodysuits, long-johns or girdles.

Don't forget: this is routine for the doctor—all in a day's work. You'll be asked for some specific details, such as what your main complaint is and how long it has bothered you; how severe the pain is; how much bleeding there is; what colour the blood is; how often you see blood or have pain; and whether it is affected by having a bowel movement. If you have pain in the anal area, the doctor will ask whether it is inside or outside the opening, or both, and whether it is all around the circle or in one spot. Is it on the left, right, top or bottom? (The pain can't be in the middle because that is open anal canal.) Do not be frustrated: it is not always easy to tell the exact location, but it is always easier if you have had a chance to think about it before your visit to the doctor.

The doctor will also ask you about any abdominal pains, your bowel habits and any family history of colon diseases, such as cancer. These are the main questions directly related to the colon and rectum.

Most doctors do not request you use a laxative or enema before a regular physical examination. However, if you do not usually have a bowel movement in the morning or tend to be constipated, it may be a good idea to use an enema (such as a Fleet enema, available at most drugstores) 1 hour before leaving for the appointment.

When Should Your Visits Start?

Your first visit to your family doctor for colon cancer prevention should be at *age 30*—earlier if you have any complaints or a family history of colon problems. This first visit should only be for a simple physical and an examination with the short scopes (anoscope and sigmoidoscope). Unfortunately, since many family physicians do not have an anoscope or a sigmoidoscope, they may need to refer you to a specialist. This could be a colorectal surgeon, a gastroenterologist or some general surgeons. Make sure that the doctor you are referred to is equipped to do a colonoscopy examination, although this is only necessary if a problem is found and for routine colon cancer prevention after age 45.

The Examination

Two positions are most commonly used. At your family doctor's, you are likely to be in the *left lateral position*: lying on the left side, covered by a sheet (see Figure 4), with knees tucked up under the chin, as in the fetal position, and bottom extending over the edge of the table.

Most specialists are likely to put you in the *knee-chest position* on a proctology table: lying on the tummy, with the edge of the table at the hips, with knee support allowing your whole body to assume the kneeling position (see Figure 5). These tables make procedures more comfortable for you and easier for the doctor, because the height and angle can be adjusted. In this position, you can be covered more easily by a sheet with a hole exposing the anal area, and nothing else. (Maybe this is where the term "bottoms up" comes from.)

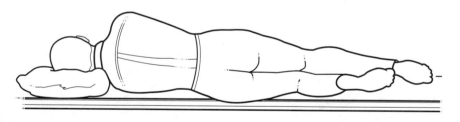

Figure 4: Left Lateral Position

No matter what position or table is used, the doctor will pull the buttocks apart for better visibility. Ideally, you do this for the doctor. Not only does this free the doctor's hands so they can hold the instrument, it also means you can control how far to pull. This is especially helpful if there is pain: you will pull more because you know you can

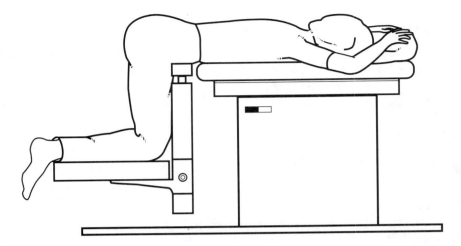

Figure 5: Knee-Chest Position

stop when the pain gets bad. Pulling the buttocks apart is important for good visibility, which the doctor needs for accurate diagnosis.

Of course, if you're nervous about the examination or have a lot of pain, the buttocks and sphincter muscles are likely to be in spasm before the doctor even gets within arm's reach. That makes it more awkward for everyone, so it is important to try to relax. Various tricks help. Check your shoulders—are they tight? If they are, so is your sphincter muscle. Take a deep breath and then let it out in a long, slow sigh. Tell the doctor a story—about your dream trip to Hawaii or your last vacation. Try trading jokes with the doctor—chances are, you will both know a few, as there are plenty of stories about this specialty.

During the *visual examination,* the doctor will look for irritation of the skin, then for skin tags, a fissure or fistula and any swellings and growths. The doctor will see if there is a protrusion such as a pile or a polyp coming down from the anal canal (another reason to pull the buttocks far apart).

After this visual examination comes the *digital examination.* Wearing gloves, the doctor lubricates a finger and the anal canal with some water-soluble lubricant, then slowly inserts the finger through the anal canal and into the lower rectum. Be sure to speak up if you have any pain in the anal area, so the doctor can go slower.

The digital examination offers many clues to anorectal health. For example, pain experienced when a finger is inserted into the anal canal may indicate anusitis. Pain in only one spot might indicate a fissure. The doctor feels all around the anal canal for any swelling before advancing up into the rectum. In men, the doctor can feel the prostate, but this is not a very effective way to check it because most of the prostate grows in the other direction. (Besides, the PSA blood test and ultrasound are better for examining the prostate.) In women, the doctor can feel the cervix and a bit of the uterus (womb); it's also possible to feel for a rectocele (bulge of the rectum into the vagina). The doctor checks the state of the sphincter muscles by inserting a gloved finger into the anal canal and then asking you to tighten your sphincter muscles.

Sometimes the doctor does a *bidigital examination*, examining the anal canal with both index fingers at the same time. As one finger is pulled half way out, the other is inserted. Each finger is advanced a little at a time as far as it will go. As they are both slowly withdrawn at the same time, the fingertips are continuously bent and straightened towards the side. This allows the doctor to feel any constricting ring or band of scar tissue in the anal canal (anal stenosis). Anal stenosis is one of the two most frequently missed anal diagnoses (the other is anusitis). The bidigital examination should be done on the first visit and then every 2 to 3 years—not on each visit.

The next step after the digital examination is to look up into the anal canal and rectum with either an anoscope or a sigmoidoscope, or both. These examinations usually require a referral to a specialist, if the family physician does not have the equipment, and are necessary if there is any pain or swelling encountered during the digital examination, or if there is a history of bleeding or another complaint low in the rectum.

The *anoscope* is a short, tapered, hollow tube, narrowing at the tip, with a light shining through it (see Figure 6). It is shorter and easier to use than a sigmoidoscope and requires no preparation since it allows inspection only of the anal canal. The doctor looks through the anoscope and sees the inside of the anal canal and lowest part of the rectum—the area felt by the finger.

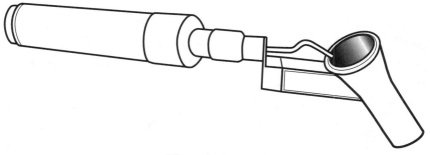

Figure 6: Anoscope

The anoscope has a removable insert that fills in the leading edge of the scope. The doctor lubricates the tip and gently inserts it into the anal canal, which is also lubricated, all the way up to the rectum. This is the moment for you to give a good long sigh, to relax the sphincter muscle.

When the scope is all the way in, the lower rectum can be inspected for any abnormalities. Then the scope is slowly withdrawn until its far edge is at the dentate line, where the doctor can look for piles or swellings or signs of irritation. Visibility is better on the way out than it is on the way in; removing the anoscope slowly gives the doctor a clear view of the anal canal.

Next, the doctor uses a *rigid sigmoidoscope* to check the rectum for inflammation or growths. The sigmoidoscope is like an extension of the anoscope. It is a rigid tube 1 foot (25 cm) long, with a light in the handle that transmits right through fibre optics to the other end (see Figure 7). It has a removable insert and a glass window at the handle end which acts as a magnifier and protects the doctor's eyes. It may be reassuring for you to know that the outer end of this scope is closed off; there can be no accidents.

The sigmoidoscope is inserted as far as it will go without causing too much discomfort. The further it goes, the more area can be examined; in some people, there is a sharp bend where the rectum meets the sigmoid colon, so in them it can only go in about 6 inches (15 cm). Once the sigmoidoscope is in place, you will feel as though gas or stool is present. With the glass window closed, the doctor can insert a small amount of air to distend (swell) the rectum by squeezing an attached balloon. This provides a better view. As with the anoscope, visibility is best on withdrawal, so the doctor will pull the scope out slowly, to be sure not to miss anything. The whole procedure only takes a minute or so to complete.

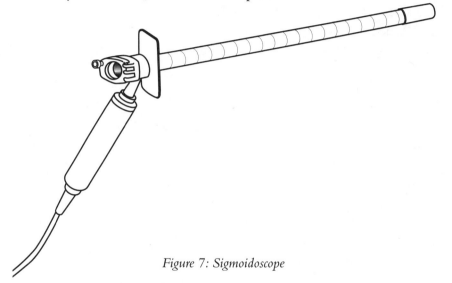

Figure 7: Sigmoidoscope

The sigmoidoscope is the best instrument for examining the rectum. The doctor can examine the lining to make sure that it is not inflamed and there are no growths. Polyps and tumours occur in the rectum at least as frequently as in other parts of the colon, so it is very important that you receive a sigmoidoscopy examination at least every 2 years from the age of 30. After age 45, you should alternate it with colonoscopy examinations.

Doctors sometimes use a *flexible sigmoidoscope*. Unlike the shorter, rigid sigmoidoscope, this is a flexible instrument just over 2 feet (65 cm) long; it can reveal more lesions because it goes farther up the bowel. It isn't used much by specialists—a colonoscope goes all the way through the entire colon and reveals even more.

Some doctors still use the *barium enema x-ray*, although, in most instances, colonoscopy is much more accurate. X-ray may be useful when colonoscopy all the way up to the cecum (the uppermost part of the colon) is not possible. It should always be done if the colonoscope is not available, although colonoscopy shows three times more lesions than an x-ray does.

What the x-ray does best is give an overall picture of the outline of the colon, but this information is rarely required. The x-ray may expose an irregular pattern of the lining (mucosa) and the colon wall. Diverticula (balloon-like pouches), which start from the inside and extend through the wall of the colon, show up well on an x-ray. Both also show up on colonoscopy.

A barium enema x-ray is done by a radiologist, who inserts a tube into the rectum and injects barium fluid through the tube into the rectum. As more barium mixed with air is added, it pushes the fluid through the rest of the colon. Using only barium may create a dense white mass ("whiteout") that makes smaller lesions easy to miss. Most radiologists add some air in what is called an *air contrast study*. The added air gives better detail but may be quite uncomfortable for the person. However, it doesn't last long. After you've had several x-rays taken, you go to the toilet, for instant relief. After evacuation, one last x-ray is taken.

Warning: If a few days pass without a bowel movement, the barium sitting in the colon may dry out and become like concrete. Most radiologists advise taking a laxative if there has been no bowel movement by the next day. Don't let more than 2 days pass without a bowel movement. Bulk formers, such as high-fibre cereals, are good to take right after a barium enema x-ray. And keep in mind that bowel action always takes a day or two to return to normal after a strong laxative—there isn't anything left to come out. It takes time to build up.

One limitation of the barium enema x-ray is that it does not provide a direct view of the colon. It is a black-and-white picture that shows only shadows. In fact, if the x-ray shows a lesion, the doctor has to do a colonoscopy anyway (which has the added advantage that most growths can then be removed on the spot). A strong laxative is necessary the night before the examination to clean out all the stool from the colon, because any traces of stool leave shadows in the picture that may look like a growth or hide one. A questionable or wrong diagnosis sometimes occurs on x-ray, which might lead to an unnecessary operation, as was the case for a young man whose three separate x-ray studies showed a consistent "polyp" in the same spot. It turned out to be an air bubble. Given the option, always choose colonoscopy.

There are other disadvantages to a barium enema x-ray. First, a small but unavoidable amount of radiation is involved. Second, if anything abnormal is found, another clean-out with laxatives is required before a colonoscopy examination to test or remove the lesion.

Colonoscopy is by far the best way to examine the entire colon and even as far as a few inches of the small bowel. It reveals much more detail in colour, which can expose three times as many lesions as an x-ray or flexible sigmoidoscopy. Also, it allows the doctor to take a biopsy (sample) of a lesion or remove it altogether. Especially with the new colonoscopes, much smaller lesions can be found and removed—an important factor in cancer prevention.

Not until recently has it been proven that all colon cancers come from polyps. Most colon cancer can thus be prevented by removing polyps (*polypectomy*) before they turn malignant—one of the most important messages in this book. Here is where colonoscopy shines. The doctor can check the whole length of the colon and remove most polyps in the same examination. No need to book another appointment, take another laxative and go through the procedure a second time. In fact, in many cases, an abdominal operation is avoided.

However, using a colonoscope, especially to remove a lesion, requires both special training and experience, which can take some time to acquire. This is usually not an examination done by a family physician. The experienced colonoscopist can reach the cecum quickly, causing little, if any, pain—just some cramping that occurs as the scope advances around a corner. The cramps, lasting only a few seconds, indicate progress. The examination is more difficult for someone who is nervous, has a history of severe constipation or has a floppy, redundant colon.

As with the barium enema x-ray, bowel preparation is very important: a thorough clean-out with laxatives. The examination is useless if the field is not clear.

Most colonoscopes are 5 to 7 feet long (125 to 175 cm). There are two kinds: fibre optic and video. The *fibre-optic colonoscope* has 40,000 small individual fibres running from one end of the scope to the other. Light passes from the head end of the scope through the fibres and lights up the inside of the colon as the scope bends around corners. Another bundle of fibres brings the image back for the doctor to see. It is like looking into a flexible periscope that magnifies the image five times. This enables the doctor to pass the scope up inside the colon, go around the corners and still see the inside of the colon directly—all in living colour!

The *video colonoscope* is the latest (and very expensive) development in colon examinations. A video chip inside the tip of the scope transmits a picture to a video monitor (see Figure 8). The high-quality, high-definition picture is magnified 4 to 10 times. More polyps are found using the video colonoscope, which means more potential cancers are prevented.

Using either a fibre-optic or a video colonoscope, the doctor inspects the lining of the colon to see if it is inflamed or abnormal in any way. There might be diverticula (especially in the sigmoid colon) or bleeding, or there might be growths such as polyps or more serious tumours.

Certain landmarks indicate where the tip of the scope is located in the colon. It starts at the *anal canal*, which is normally collapsed (empty). From there, it enters the lowest part of the *rectum*, which is an open tube that acts as a reservoir for stool. The lining of the rectum is pale, and the blood vessels in its wall stand out clearly. The whole rectum is only 6 inches (15 cm) long.

The rectum leads to the *sigmoid* colon, which can move around inside the abdominal cavity because it is attached by a *mesentery* (like an apron, with the sigmoid colon attached along the three sides). This mesentery carries the blood vessels that travel to and from the bowel. Water absorbed from the colon travels through the mesentery's veins to the liver. As a result, the sigmoid colon is easily stretched into a big loop by the scope.

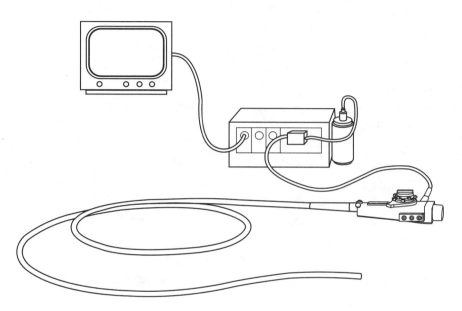

Figure 8: Video Colonoscope

Next, the scope advances into the *descending* colon. Unlike the sigmoid colon, the descending colon is fixed along the back wall of the abdomen on the left side. It is a relatively straight tube that leads up to the left side of the ribcage and ends at the bend (*splenic flexure*). From there, the scope enters the *transverse* colon, which crosses the abdomen under the ribcage from left to right and has a characteristic triangular appearance. It is sometimes possible to see the pulsations of the *aorta* (blood vessel that distributes blood from the heart). Like the sigmoid colon, the transverse colon is attached loosely to the back wall by a long mesentery and is moveable and floppy. It can also be distended into a large loop, which then travels all the way down from the left side of the ribcage to the very bottom of the abdomen and then all the way back up to the right side of the ribcage. Because of this great length, the transverse colon often takes more of the scope. In this situation, at both ends of the transverse colon, the two angles are sharp, which makes them difficult to pass the scope through, so the colonoscopist tries to keep the freely moving parts of the colon as straight as possible.

At the junction of the transverse and the *ascending* colon, it is possible to see the blue-brown reflection of the liver—an excellent landmark. The ascending colon is also fixed to the back wall along the right side, just as the descending colon is on the back wall along the left side.

At the end is the *cecum*, into which the small bowel empties through the *ileocecal valve*. Nearby is the base of the appendix, which looks like a half moon with a central slit. These are the final landmarks, indicating the end of the trip.

The dictum "advance to arrive and withdraw to see" is even more true in colonoscopy than in the other examinations. All these details are much more clearly seen on the way out because the tip of the scope can be more easily kept away from the wall on withdrawal.

One thing many people find interesting about colonoscopy is that they can look at the inside of their own colon. If the doctor is using a fibre-optic colonoscope, ask to take a peek; with video colonoscopy, you can watch the whole procedure on the monitor. While you are at it, check how well you're cleaned out. You'll realize how much easier it is to see these landmarks as well as any polyps, especially small ones, when the colon is clean.

Most people have very few abdominal pains or cramps after a colonoscopy as long as whatever air was inserted into the colon has been removed on the way out. Once they're active, they will start passing gas again. Any irritation of the anal skin from having so many bowel movements because of the laxative will also quickly disappear.

After the examination, you may start eating right away. But start with light foods for a few hours. You'll put on any weight lost while taking the laxative once you start drinking fluids.

A Word about Laxatives and Preparing for a Colonoscopy

The biggest complaint about a colonoscopy is not the procedure itself but the laxative required the night before. With a good laxative, you no longer need to go without food for as long as you used to. After a light lunch the day before the examination, you can still have clear fluids such as clear soups (broth), juices (apple), non-carbonated drinks and clear Jell-O (but not red Jell-O, as it may be mistaken for blood).

If you really hate to go without food, you can take a food supplement, such as Ensure. No one has to fast for 2 to 3 days before the exam any more.

The most recommended laxatives are Citro-Mag (magnesium citrate) and Phosphosoda. (Golightly is another good one, but most people are put off by the large volume it mixes up into.) Take one bottle of Citro-Mag or Phosphosoda at 6 o'clock the night before the examination. It will be easier if the liquid is cold. Pour it into a glass filled with ice and drink it slowly or quickly, whichever you prefer. Make sure to follow it with a glass of room-temperature water every 15 minutes until you have had six full glasses. The water is needed to flush out the system. Drink the second bottle at 8 p.m.

How do you know if the laxative has worked well? There should be no more solid stool, only a little fluid that is clear or has a brown tinge. You will probably have gone to the toilet 10 to 15 times. If the clean-out was not complete or there is a history of constipation, it may be necessary to take a third bottle of laxative the morning of the examination.

Some people are nauseated by the laxatives. In such cases, I recommend taking Gravol half an hour before each bottle of laxative. Occasionally, some people have abdominal cramps similar to those accompanying severe diarrhea, which are relieved when the bowel movements begin.

Sedatives and Pain Relief

Some people are quite nervous, especially if it is their first colonoscopy. I advise anyone who is at all apprehensive to ask the doctor for
sedation. Usually, a small amount of Demerol, for pain relief, and some
Versed, a tranquillizer, are injected. This combination takes effect—and
is most effective—almost immediately. You must not drive for 6 to 8
hours after the injection, although you may take public transit or a taxi
after about 1 hour.

It is extremely important to tell the doctor in advance if you are
allergic to any of these drugs, if you have a history of heart-valve problems or prostheses, or if you have had an artificial joint replacement
within the past year. In these cases, antibiotics should be taken before
the procedure. Never take any other medication, such as other tran-
quillizers, before a procedure without first consulting the doctor.

For the best colorectal health, I strongly recommend that the
colonoscopy be repeated 2 years later, with a sigmoidoscopy during
the year in between. (The rectum is seen better with the shorter sigmoidoscope.) If a polyp, especially a large, benign one, is found and
removed during a colonoscopy, cancer has possibly been prevented.
A repeat examination is recommended in a year for these cases. But
even a small, cancerous tumour can be removed during colonoscopy
if the cancer is limited to the tip of the polyp. If it has extended to the
base, then the cancer can be treated by surgical resection. That's why
a routine of colonoscopies, with a sigmoidoscopy in between, in
which any polyps are removed, is ideal. Usually, if this routine is followed, the worst tumours are found mostly on the first visit; in the
rare instances that a cancerous polyp is found during a follow-up examination, it is usually small and easily curable, which may be why
people feel more relaxed for subsequent colonoscopies. A very fast-
growing kind of cancer spreads beyond the bowel wall to other organs, rather than growing on the inside of the bowel, where it would

be visible on colonoscopy; fortunately, this kind of cancer, which is not preventable, is very rare. In fact, I have only seen it three times in 25,000 colonoscopies. If no polyps are found on the second colonoscopy, I don't recommend another for 3 years. The longest I would go between colonoscopies is 5 years.

HIV/AIDS and the Doctor's Office

After the media reported a few cases of HIV transmitted by a dentist to his patients, many people were afraid of getting the virus, which is linked to AIDS, at the dentist's or doctor's office.

It turned out that this dentist wasn't washing his instruments properly in soap and water, let alone disinfecting them.

Some time later, a U.S. government study was conducted to assess the effectiveness of cleaning solutions, and the best ones were determined. This was also widely reported in the press and blown out of proportion.

The fear these reports created is exemplified by a call we received at the Rudd Clinic from a woman asking if she was at risk because her "doctor had died of AIDS"; he had, in fact, died of lung cancer, not AIDS. The concern is justified because, once the virus is acquired, death from AIDS occurs in most cases—but need we be terrified?

To be sure, AIDS is a widespread, plague-like illness. It is estimated that three million North Americans have already contracted the virus linked to AIDS and that many more millions are infected in other, less developed countries, such as Africa. In parts of Africa, where the disease probably originated, the number of people infected is much greater, as is the death rate.

This is devastating and does not bode well for the future of the North American economy (among other things), where the disease is at an earlier stage. We don't appreciate the seriousness of the problem because the virus can take years to develop into full-blown AIDS. The worst aspect is that it affects mostly young people—the ones who are the most productive in our economy.

The first case of AIDS was diagnosed as recently as 1981. It probably started in Africa and was transmitted by a monkey. Until recently, the incidence of AIDS almost doubled every year in the United States. This alarming statistic prompted a media campaign (even more extensive in Europe) intended to frighten people, particularly gays and sexually active young people, into using safe-sex techniques. A great deal of effort has also been spent on explaining to intravenous drug users and healthcare workers the dangers of infected needles and syringes and the proper techniques for disinfecting instruments and for safe waste disposal. However, it is important to realize that this disease could infect almost anyone.

What is AIDS?

AIDS is the result of being infected by the human immunodeficiency virus (HIV). The virus attacks the blood cells (*T-lymphocytes*) that make up the immune system of the body. When the immune system is damaged, there are not enough T-lymphocyte cells to fight certain infections caused by bacteria and viruses that are normally present but not harmful. Because of the immune system's inability to police and capture these bacteria and abnormal cells, they multiply freely without interference. Certain types of pneumonia and cancers of the lung and skin, which are not commonly seen otherwise, can occur. People don't actually die from AIDS or HIV; they die from the infections and cancers that are the result of this devastating virus's effect on the immune system.

HIV lives in the blood, semen and secretions of an infected person. To infect another person, the virus must penetrate the skin or mucous membrane, through a cut or break in the skin, in the lining of the mouth or in the lining of the rectum or vagina. Casual touching or social contact, such as a handshake or a kiss on the cheek, will not infect anyone. HIV is not contracted from toilet seats or door handles.

By far the most frequently infected are intravenous drug users and the sexually active, particularly homosexuals, especially through anal intercourse. *Intravenous drug users* get the virus from sharing infected needles to inject drugs directly into their veins. When a person injects a needle, the plunger of the syringe is pulled back to make sure the needle is in the vein. After the injection, some of the blood drawn into the syringe remains when the plunger is pulled back. This blood could be infected with HIV, which can survive a day or two in the blood in the syringe. If this syringe is used by someone else, the virus is injected directly into that person's bloodstream. There isn't any contact more intimate than this—blood to blood. This is why all healthcare professionals—doctors, dentists, nurses—use only disposable syringes and needles.

As a *sexually transmitted virus*, HIV is spread in two ways—anal intercourse and promiscuity (both bisexual and homosexual). *Anal intercourse* is much riskier than vaginal intercourse. The lining of the anal canal is very easily irritated, inflamed and torn, leaving a window open for the virus to enter. Anal intercourse is usually more forceful than vaginal intercourse and often causes a break in the lining of the anal canal, as is evident from the frequent spotting of blood afterwards. Infected semen has a great opportunity to pass in through this window. This can happen among homosexuals and heterosexuals, but because anal intercourse is more frequent among gays, HIV and AIDS are more common among them, too.

Promiscuity is also a factor among gays, since some have many sexual partners. Having many sexual partners has spread the virus to many people over a short period of time. This is why so many health and government agencies advocate monogamy—having only one sexual partner in both homosexual and heterosexual relationships. The trend towards one sexual partner and the practice of safe sex will likely be the reasons for any decrease in the incidence of AIDS in the near future.

Oral sex and deep kissing are, indeed, intimate contact, but unlike anal intercourse these do not usually cause any cuts or tears, so HIV is not as easily transmitted. However, there is a small risk of transmission if the mucous membrane of the mouth and the tongue are raw, perhaps as a result of biting the tongue or gingivitis. This is why safe-sex techniques include the recommendation that men wear a condom during oral sex.

The incidence of AIDS is now on the rise among women. This is possibly due to an increase in anal and vaginal intercourse with male partners who have themselves had anal intercourse. *Vaginal intercourse* does not present a high risk because the vaginal lining is much tougher than that of the anal canal and is less easily damaged by intercourse. Also, the vagina is much larger and more flexible, whereas the anal canal is narrower, being surrounded by a strong muscle. For these reasons, there is much less chance of a break occurring in the lining of the vagina and of transmitting HIV by only vaginal intercourse.

Most of us have heard stories in the news recently about problems with infected blood used in *blood transfusions*. Blood used in the 1980s was not tested for HIV. Now, sophisticated testing is carried out before any transfusion is given. Also, fewer transfusions are given, especially during elective surgery, and much less blood is used. Special care is taken to avoid transmitting viruses such as HIV or hepatitis, and researchers are looking at new kinds of artificial blood for use in transfusions and heart surgery. In some cases, it is possible for a person to have blood drawn several weeks before elective surgery; the blood is stored and then used during the surgery if necessary. Or blood is donated by a close relative or friend whose blood has been tested.

It is tragic when HIV is transmitted from an HIV-positive mother to her child. This can occur not only during pregnancy, labour and delivery but also from breastfeeding. This occurs in 12 to 30% of all cases. An infected baby has a poor prognosis.

The Risk of Getting AIDS from the Doctor or Dentist

Spreading the virus is a potential problem at the doctor's or dentist's office, but, if reasonable precautions are taken, it should not happen. That's one reason why all dentists and many doctors now wear gloves and masks.

The main concern is to ensure there are no blood clots or secretions that can keep the virus alive. This is why it is so important to wash away blood or body fluids carefully, especially in hard-to-reach places such as the hinges or internal parts of instruments. Good old-fashioned mechanical cleaning with brushes and soap and water does the trick in preparation for disinfecting.

Although it is not enough to rely solely on disinfectants, new ones are available that kill infective agents as quickly and effectively as the much more expensive and time-consuming steam and gas sterilization. This is fortunate because some of the newer equipment is too fragile to be put in a steam sterilizer (which is also very expensive for an office practice).

Of course, disinfecting agents have to kill different kinds of infective agents, such as bacteria, parasites, spores, fungi and viruses. The spores are the toughest to kill because they are completely covered by a protective layer. The disinfecting solutions must kill the spores within a few minutes. By that time, the viruses are long since dead. The viruses, which are very fragile—much more fragile than bacteria, are the easiest to kill. Survival outside the body is brief—only a few seconds. HIV is quickly killed by air, and it is instantly killed by a simple disinfectant such as ordinary household bleach diluted nine times. However, it can survive up to 2 days outside the body in a blood clot. The virus that most people don't even think about is the hepatitis virus—it is a hundred times easier to be infected by hepatitis than by HIV. But if the spores can be killed, then the viruses can certainly be killed. The bottom line is that the virus linked to AIDS is very easily killed by air and certainly by disinfecting solutions, provided the instruments are properly cleaned. It means going back to scrubbing properly with soap and water—"back to the future." As long as the doctors and dentists clean the instruments well, a good disinfecting solution will do the rest.

Healthcare workers must be extra-careful whenever any procedure they are doing results in a break in the skin or mucosal lining. This, of course, occurs whenever there is any bleeding, when there is some discharge of body fluids, such as saliva, semen and rectal secretions, and with all injections.

Doctors, nurses and especially dentists, who work with drills, can easily get blood splattered into their eyes or onto their fingers, where they may have a small abrasion that they are not aware of. They must be careful not to be cut by a knife or pricked by a needle while treating a person with HIV. Some even wear two pairs of gloves. Even though many healthcare workers have been pricked by needles while working on infected people, only a few have actually contracted the virus. The one or two who have become ill have created a sensational media story.

There are some doctors who are HIV-positive. This poses a controversial and difficult problem. Some would like to have these doctors banned from treating people entirely. However, this is probably not necessary, providing extra precautions are taken. Even so, it is probably best that HIV-positive healthcare workers not work in high-risk jobs where there might be contact with blood or body fluids.

Needles, Syringes and Injections

Not too many years ago, doctors and nurses used and reused glass syringes and needles at the office, on house calls and in the hospital. The needles would even be sharpened. These should never be used. To avoid possible infection, only disposable syringes and needles should be used. This also means that the needle is always sharp. Extra care must be taken in the proper disposal of needles and syringes so that the handlers are protected.

These procedures are now used all over North America; however, it is important to keep them in mind when travelling, particularly to places that might not have as up-to-date standards.

Drugs and Vaccines for HIV/AIDS—The Future?

A few drugs are already in use which will help some people with some of the complications of AIDS, such as pneumonia, and temporarily keep the virus in check. The emphasis has changed lately and a lot of effort is going into searching for drugs that will attack the virus directly or boost the immune system.

The most exciting search going on now is for a vaccine to prevent HIV infection in the first place. One research group from the University of California at Los Angeles (UCLA) claims to have created a decoy virus which looks physically and acts chemically like HIV. When injected into the body, the immune system is fooled into creating an antibody against the virus. Unfortunately, these very laborious and expensive processes, once developed, need years of field testing to prove they work and are safe. Bureaucratic government agencies, in trying to do their job, often delay approval of a new drug for years, increasing the time and cost of producing it. It can cost more than one-hundred million dollars to bring a new drug onto the market. No wonder these new drugs are so expensive.

As if they didn't have enough challenges, one of the greatest problems researchers face is that since HIV readily changes or mutates into another form of the virus, the original drug or vaccine becomes ineffective. With all these problems and costs, the cure for AIDS may be years away.

2

Constipation and Outflow Problems

C ONSTIPATION is so common in the "civilized" Western culture that at least 50% of the population in England have reportedly taken laxatives at one time or another.

By contrast, in the "primitive" culture of the tribes in rural Africa, constipation is practically unheard of. This fact has been studied by Dr. D. Burkitt and Dr. N. S. Painter from Great Britain, who discovered that the Africans studied had almost no colon cancer, appendicitis, diverticulitis or hemorrhoids. Yet we have a much higher incidence of these. They have 2 to 3 large bowel movements a day, whereas we may have one every 2 to 3 days. Analyzing the Africans' diets, Burkitt and Painter learned that the main difference was fibre. In fact, the two researchers are responsible for reintroducing fibre into our diet, although few people realize how important fibre is, even now. Fewer know that there are two different kinds of fibre.

Since several different conditions are often mistakenly identified by the term constipation, before we talk about diet and fibre or how long to spend on the toilet, let's discuss the difference between true and false constipation.

What is Constipation?

To determine whether constipation is true or false, we ask two questions: Does the stool come right down into the rectum but won't come out? Or does the stool not get down into the rectum in the first place? "True" *constipation* occurs when little stool reaches the rectum; *outflow obstruction* ("false" constipation) occurs when the stool in the rectum will not come out without a lot of pushing or straining. These problems must be diagnosed separately because each requires different treatment.

What is the norm? One to three large, bulky, soft but firm bowel movements per day.

The person with constipation has too few and too small bowel movements and typically pushes and strains to try to get out what's there. Lots of time may be spent on the toilet. The "regular" person is in and out of the bathroom within 2 minutes. A tendency towards constipation is present if a day goes by without a bowel movement, if the stool is hard and dry, or if it is small and pebbly or like rabbit stools.

Constipation is usually due to insufficient bulk in the stool, caused by lack of fibre or water in the diet. Other causes include lack of exercise, metabolic imbalances, such as changes in the thyroid, or different levels of hormones during pregnancy or menstruation. Stress, loss of body fluids in hot weather and excessive perspiration may also be factors.

On examining the abdomen, the doctor can sometimes feel if there is a lot of stool in the colon. If there's a history of abdominal cramps, the doctor may listen to the bowel sounds with a stethoscope. Some gurgling is normal, too much is not. If this is increased in number, intensity and pitch, it suggests a blockage higher up.

One factor in preventing constipation is *physical activity*. The sedentary person who gets no exercise or someone whose physical abilities are limited will have more problems with constipation. An active person tends to have more regular bowel habits; an inactive person often has an inactive bowel. Therefore, the constipated person should make a point of exercising. The best anti-constipation exercises strengthen the abdominal muscles: e.g., abdominal crunches (lie on your back with your legs bent and your hands behind your neck; raise your head and shoulders, keeping the back flat on the ground). Touching the toes and energetic walking are also good exercises.

Fibre

Our great-grandparents were almost never constipated. This is because they ate 50 to 60 g of fibre a day. Today, most of us eat only 10 g a day. The ideal amount is at least 35; people with severe constipation may need as much as 45 g. Our great-grandparents used stone-ground flour and unrefined sugar in their cooking and baking. We eat so much prepared food, refined so that it has almost no fibre. We eat white sugar, white bread and flour, steaks, hamburgers, French fries and other fast-food items that have almost no fibre at all. It is almost impossible for us to eat 30 to 40 g of fibre a day on this type of diet without resorting to fibre supplements.

There are two types of fibre—soluble and insoluble. *Soluble fibre* is absorbed through the lining of the bowel into the bloodstream. This type of fibre is thought to lower the blood fats and cholesterol; it doesn't stay in the bowel, however, so it doesn't help constipation. One example of soluble fibre is the oat bran we were told not so long ago is good for the heart. Another example is psyllium seed, which is in many products, including Metamucil. Although Metamucil is usually promoted for constipation, I understand that it consists of 90% soluble fibre, which is absorbed into the bloodstream, and only 10% insoluble fibre, which stays in the bowel. That means you have to take an awful lot of psyllium to help constipation.

Insoluble fibre does not pass through the bowel wall but stays within the colon. It adds bulk to the stool by absorbing water to the fibre. A well-known example of insoluble fibre is wheat bran, which is 90% insoluble and is a good additive to use.

Fibre can be taken in many forms, but the best by far is high–fibre cereal. It's best to eat foods high in fibre and take 35 g of fibre a day. Start by getting out of the habit of eating white bread. Whole-wheat bread has about 1.3 g per slice—so even five slices of whole-wheat bread a day will provide 6.5 g of fibre. Cereals usually have the fibre content printed on the label; there are cereals on the market with much higher fibre content than the popular ones most of us eat. Aim for 13 to 15 g of insoluble fibre in each bowl of cereal.

But no matter what kind of fibre you eat, it does no good for the bowel unless water is drunk with it. To create bulk requires *water*— not tea or coffee or juice, just plain water—at the same time the fibre is eaten. Many people don't know this; they may be constipated despite the added bran in their diets, because they aren't drinking enough water with it. Unless they are accompanied by water, there is no use taking bran or eating foods high in fibre—they may actually cause constipation. Always drink two glasses of water while and after eating a high-fibre food, e.g., cereal, and one glass with whole-wheat bread, potatoes with their skins on or carrots.

Here are a few useful things to remember:

- Fibre is a chemical substance that you cannot see. It is not strands or threads that you can see.
- The insoluble form of fibre prevents constipation because it remains inside the bowel, where it is needed.
- Fibre acts by absorbing water and swelling up to create bulk inside the bowel.

Fibre content in fruits and vegetables

Foods	Grams of Insoluble Fibre (Approx.)
Fruits (raw)	
Raspberries, ¾ cup (187 mL)	6.4
Strawberries, 1 cup (250 mL)	4.0
Blackberries, ½ cup (125 mL)	3.9
Orange, 1	3.0
Apple, 1	2.0
Pear, ½ medium	2.0
Grapefruit, ½ cup (125 mL)	1.1
Kiwi, 1	1.0
Beans	
Green, 1 cup (250 mL)	4.0
White, ½ cup (125 mL)	3.6
Kidney, ½ cup (125 mL)	3.3
Pinto, ½ cup (125 mL)	3.3
Lima, ½ cup (125 mL)	3.2
Vegetables	
Potato with skin, baked, 1 large	4.0
Squash, acorn, ½ cup (125 mL)	3.8
Peas, ½ cup (125 mL)	3.0
Corn, creamed canned, ½ cup (125 mL)	2.7
Brussels sprouts, ½ cup (125 mL)	2.3
Asparagus, ¾ cup (187 mL)	2.3
Corn, kernels, ½ cup (125 mL)	2.1
Zucchini, ½ cup (125 mL)	1.4
Carrots, cooked, ½ cup (125 mL)	1.2
Broccoli, ½ cup (125 mL)	1.1

Fibre content in grains and cereals

Foods	Grams of Insoluble Dietary Fibre (Approx.)
Cold Cereals	
Fibre First, ½ cup (30 g)	15.0
Fibre One, ½ cup (30 g)	12.8
All Bran, ½ cup (30 g)	10.0
Raisin Bran, ¾ cup (40 g)	4.6
Bran Flakes, 1 cup (30 g)	4.4
Shreddies, ⅔ cup (30 g)	2.7
Cheerios, 1 cup (30 g)	2.2
Corn Flakes, 1 ¼ cup (30 g)	0.8
Frosted Flakes, ¾ cup (30 g)	0.5
Special K, 1 ¼ cup (30 g)	0.4
Rice Krispies, 1 ¼ cup (30 g)	0.3
Hot Cereals	
Oatmeal, 1 cup (48 g)	5.0
Red River cereal, ¼ cup (40 g)	5.0
Cream of wheat, 28 g	1.3
Breads	
Rye, 1 slice	2.0
Pumpernickel, 1 slice	2.0
12-grain, 1 slice	1.7
100% whole-wheat, 1 slice	1.3
Raisin, 1 slice	1.0
Cracked-wheat, 1 slice	1.0
White	0
Crackers	
Triscuit, 7 crackers	3.2
100% stoned wheat crackers, 1 oz (28 g)	3.0

Graham, 2 squares	2.3
Thin wheat crackers, I oz (28 g)	2.0
Ritz crackers	0
Saltines or soda crackers	0

Rice

Brown, cooked, I cup (195 g)	3.0
Converted white, cooked, I cup (175 g)	1.0
Long-grain white, cooked, I cup (205 g)	1.0

Supplement

Wheat bran, 3 tbsp. (9 g)	4.4

Here is the routine I recommend for a high-fibre diet:

1. Look for *cereals* with at least 10 g of dietary fibre per serving. There are several high-fibre cereals on the market, such as Fibre First, Fibre One and All Bran—but read the labels on the box to be sure you have the right one: the higher the better. Always try to eat 100% whole-wheat bread. White bread has no fibre and adds no bulk at all. Use whole-wheat flour and unrefined brown sugar in cooking and baking. Always have a glass or two of water with the fibre.

2. Eat lots of *vegetables and fruits* with a high fibre content. These include beans (legumes), raw carrots, beets, celery, lettuce and root vegetables. Eat the (washed) skin of fruit and potatoes. As when eating other high-fibre foods, it is important to drink water with them.

3. Many people may need to augment this diet with a supplement of extra fibre. A good inexpensive supplement is the natural *wheat bran* available at the supermarket or health-food store. It adds almost no calories—just bulk. The only problem is that wheat bran is too dry to eat by itself. Eating

one wheat-bran muffin a day is a good idea. Wheat bran can also be added to meatloaf and stews. The amount may vary from 1 to 4 tablespoons per day, according to your needs to get good bowel habits. Three tablespoons of wheat bran contain 4.4 g of dietary fibre. Bloating may occur, but it is only temporary. If it is bothersome, start off with 1 tablespoon a day for 1 week and gradually increase to the amount you need to have one good bowel movement a day. Always drink a glass of water while and after taking the wheat bran. Milk, coffee, juice and soda are not substitutes for water.

How to Take Wheat Bran

Wheat bran tastes like sawdust unless it is used properly. Here are three good ways of moistening wheat bran:

- Put 1 or 2 tablespoons of wheat bran in a tall glass of orange juice and mix well; wait a few minutes and then stir again and drink. Continue stirring and drinking until you've drunk it all.
- Add 1 or 2 tablespoons of wheat bran to the milk in a cereal bowl; mix and let sit for 5 minutes. Add your favourite hot or cold cereal, stir well and eat.
- Mix 1 or 2 tablespoons in (low-fat) yogurt and eat.

If you wish to lose some weight, take the cereal or wheat bran half an hour before the biggest meal of the day and follow it with a glass of water. You will probably feel full, eat less and lose weight. The more fibre you eat, the less your intake of fat.

Bowel Habits and Laxatives

True constipation tends to be a family trait; it is more prevalent in women—like mother, like daughter. It may be affected by hormonal changes during the menstrual cycle. Over the years, many people develop very bad bowel habits that are both harmful and hard to correct. However, it is not known how much of this is caused by poor bowel habits learned at an early age and how much is inherited.

For some, constipation develops because they do not answer the call when it comes. Consequently, the bowel routine is lost, and they develop a "lazy bowel." Very fortunate are those who "go like clockwork"—they always answer the call. What happens to people who have bad bowel habits? Pressure is brought to bear on the hemorrhoidal tissues and the lining of the bowel, and these people may develop piles, loose lining, a rectocele, hematomas, edema, skin tags, diverticula or other conditions, as well as a stretched, floppy or lazy bowel.

Good bowel habits can often be developed using the following routine. Immediately on arising in the morning (no matter what the time), drink a glass of warm water, insert a glycerine suppository into the rectum, and then make the bed and do some exercises for three or four minutes, to stimulate the bowel. Then sit on the toilet and push gently for 2 minutes; if nothing happens, leave. Do not stay on the toilet expectantly. If you do this every day for 3 to 6 months, you should be able to retrain the reflexes in your bowel so that, when you drink a glass of warm water, the colon is stimulated and a bowel movement will follow. But missing even one day from this routine can set you back weeks. Don't forget to listen to your body—whenever you have the urge to have a bowel movement, stop whatever you are doing and go immediately.

A *laxative* is any substance that promotes a bowel movement, either by stimulating the nervous and muscular mechanisms of the bowel or by causing an irritation to the lining of the colon. Generally speaking, laxatives should be avoided at all cost. In extreme cases, people can become dependent on taking laxatives for their emotional well-being.

Some commercial products that are *bulking agents* have the term *laxative* on the package, although technically they are not laxatives: e.g., Prodiem Plain, Colace and Metamucil. Dietary fibre, wheat bran and oat bran are not laxatives, either. They are bulk formers and, as such, are safe and not addictive.

Some laxatives, including a number of herbal laxatives and teas, contain *senna* or *cascara* and may cause permanent damage to the nerve and muscle supply of the bowel wall. They leave a permanent black pigment, which is absorbed into the lining. This condition, called *melanosis coli*, may result in damage that is often not reversible. Herbal teas are very popular—just make sure yours does not contain senna or cascara.

Prolonged use of *mineral oil* causes a decrease in the absorption of certain vitamins through the bowel wall. It makes the stool so soft and runny that the anal canal never stretches enough to prevent it from narrowing. The narrower the opening becomes, the more oil and laxatives are needed. This can cause anal stenosis (see pages 37–38).

Occasionally, some extra help may be needed if a person has not had a bowel movement for 5 or 6 days and/or is waiting for the regime of increased fibre and water plus exercises to start working. I recommend *glycerine suppositories,* especially if the stool is hard. One might be used in the evening and then another in the morning without harm. If that doesn't work, the next best thing is to use an *enema*, such as a Fleet enema, to empty out the rectum. In extreme cases, if a laxative is needed, it should be mild and the least disruptive, e.g., Agarol or milk of magnesia.

Outflow Obstructions

Outflow obstructions, or "false" constipation, involve a blockage that prevents the normal evacuation of stool from the rectum through the anal canal. The blockage is, therefore, very low down and entirely different from one that might occur higher up in the small or large bowel. A blockage higher up could be the result of kinking of the bowel or a tight band that cuts off the flow of stool through the bowel; either is usually a side effect from previous surgery. A blockage higher up in the colon might also (but rarely) result from a growth such as cancer or other, even rarer causes.

Several different conditions are grouped together under the heading *outflow obstruction*. All have one symptom in common: difficulty pushing a firm stool out through a narrowed anal canal (I sometimes abbreviate this to DPFSNC). This means straining. The stool comes down to the anal canal but has a hard time getting out. This condition usually develops so gradually that the person doesn't realize there is a blockage. Sometimes, people with anal fissures have so much pain that they involuntarily stop having bowel movements, to avoid stretching the fissure (see pages 99–105).

Anal Stenosis

Anal stenosis, much more frequent than all the other outflow obstructions put together, is the second most frequently missed anal diagnosis. The anal canal is narrowed and fixed and does not expand normally, which makes it difficult to push a large, firm thick stool out through it. Some narrowing is normal: the diameter may get a little smaller over the years—that's why the stools of children are much larger than those of adults. The most obvious symptom of anal stenosis is difficulty pushing a firm stool out through the narrowed anal canal. Stools that are loose or small in diameter are not hard to push through.

Unfortunately, most people, assuming this is constipation, don't realize they have a narrowing of the canal. Because it has happened so gradually, they have forgotten what a normal, large bowel movement is like, no longer having any thick stools. They sometimes get into the habit of taking laxatives regularly, to make the stool soft enough to get through the narrowing. They may not even be aware that their stools have over time become consistently narrower.

The narrowing of anal stenosis is the result of a ring of scar tissue all around the anal canal just below the dentate line and just under the skin. Scar tissue consists of fibrous bands so fixed and rigid they can't be stretched. What causes this ring of fibrous tissue is unknown, but scar tissue will develop anywhere there is irritation, e.g., in the anal canal in the presence of anusitis (see Chapter 6) or such irritating conditions as a long-standing or recurrent fissure (see pages 99–105).

Anal stenosis can also be caused by lack of use, when the canal isn't stretched regularly by a large stool, e.g., in people who have loose bowel movements or diarrhea on a regular basis over a prolonged period. The regular use of laxatives, mineral oil or herbal teas, especially those containing senna or cascara, will do the same thing. Indeed, using laxatives can perpetuate the problem, because someone with anal stenosis may think the problem is constipation and take more laxatives, creating more stenosis and thus narrowing the canal even more. The laxative just keeps the stool soft and thin so that it can pass through the narrowed canal.

Diagnosis of anal stenosis requires an examination of the anal canal with both index fingers at the same time—the *bidigital examination* (see page 9). Unfortunately, because this examination is not widely used, the condition usually goes undiagnosed.

Unlike the other causes of outflow obstruction, treatment for anal stenosis is simple: the procedure, called an *anoplasty*, restores the anal canal to its normal diameter when stretched, and can be done quickly in the doctor's office. A local anesthetic is injected at the anal margin on either side of the anal canal and directly into the scar tissue. The doctor makes two short incisions in the skin and then, holding the ring of scar tissue between clamps, divides it on both sides. The person uses a dilator (a reusable plastic stretching device) to prevent the anal canal from ever narrowing again. The dilator should be used daily beginning one week after the operation, then less frequently over the next 2 months until it is used only once a month to prevent the stenosis from recurring.

Anoplasty provides immediate relief. Many people report, at their post-operative visit, that they never knew a bowel movement could feel so good!

Spasm of the Anal Sphincter Muscle

Spasm of the anal sphincter muscle can also make it difficult to push out firm stool. This true obstruction is the result of an involuntary spasm of the sphincter muscle at the time of bearing down to have a bowel movement; the inappropriate contraction causes narrowing and prevents the stool from coming out.

At first, sphincter spasm is reversible. All it takes is learning to relax the muscle. But if spasm continues over a long time, scar tissue may form, and it becomes a fixed stenosis.

The first step is to become aware of what the muscle feels like when it is tightening. The best way to do this is to have the doctor insert a gloved finger into the anal canal and then ask the person to bear down. The doctor will point out when the muscle contracts, showing the person how to recognize this. Sometimes, trying to tighten makes the person realize it is already contracting. It takes practice bearing down again without contracting it to break the habit. Any time the sphincter muscle is contracted during defecation, the person must stop bearing down, relax and start again. This is not easy to do; sometimes, further help, using biofeedback, must be obtained.

Biofeedback involves practicing straining while a special balloon connected to a lever is placed inside the anal canal. The lever rises when the muscle is contracted. This visual aid, showing when the muscle involuntarily contracts, is helpful for learning to relax the sphincter muscles during defecation. Surgery is never required for this problem.

Pocketing of the Stool

Pocketing of the stool occurs frequently in women. The stool collects in a pocket called a *rectocele* at the lower end of the rectum rather than going out through the anal canal (see Figure 9). The bulge develops because the wall between the rectum and the vagina has been weakened by repeated childbirth, poor muscle tone or bearing down.

Pocketing is easily diagnosed by inserting a finger into the vagina. The pocket with stool in it can be felt bulging into the vagina. The bulge becomes more marked on straining. Applying finger pressure against the bulge through the vagina gives support to the recto-vaginal wall (the wall between the rectum and vagina) and often makes it easier to evacuate the stool. This in itself is a good diagnostic clue.

To restore normal bowel movements, the rectovaginal wall must be strengthened. This requires surgery by a gynecologist or colorectal surgeon in hospital under general anesthetic. Although the procedure is not very complicated nor very painful, it is important to be sure of the diagnosis and have an experienced surgeon do it to get good results. The area between the rectum and the vagina is opened, and the side walls are sewn together to obliterate the pocket. The hospital stay should last only a few days.

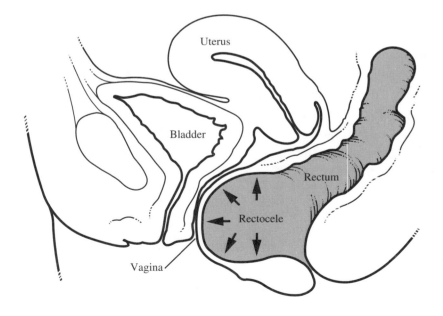

Figure 9: Rectocele

Prolapsed Rectum

A prolapsed rectum is a rare cause of outflow obstruction but an easy problem to diagnose. In a prolapsed rectum, part of the bowel comes down inside the bowel below it (see Figure 10). (Imagine the elbow of a shirt sleeve pushed down inside the sleeve and out through the cuff; the elbow of the sleeve protrudes.) At first, the bowel may not come all the way down to the outside; this is called an *intussusception* (partial prolapse). In either case, while the bowel is turned inside out on itself, a narrowing results that partially blocks the passage of stool and gives the person the full sensation of needing to have a bowel movement.

Various factors cause weakness in the muscles that hold the rectum and uterus up inside. These may be congenital or related to the way the pelvis is made. Women have a larger pelvis for birth and less support for the pelvic organs. This weakness may increase after a hysterectomy. Straining at stool is often the last straw—the prolapse may occur after a severe bout of constipation or after continuous straining at stool.

The person usually starts mistaking a feeling of fullness inside the rectum for constipation. There may be a little bleeding or mucus discharge, or both, and a partial blockage to evacuation. When fully prolapsed, the rectum protrudes right outside. Typically the size of a lemon, rounded and symmetrical, it is not a swelling on just one side of the canal (like a hematoma) nor is it very painful.

The diagnosis is easily made from this characteristic appearance. The only problem during the visit to the doctor is that the person must be able to push it out (usually this is best done in the washroom) so that the doctor can see it. It's always hard to diagnose something you can't see!

In the early stage of intussusception, when the rectum is not yet outside, the diagnosis must be made by *defecography*: a video x-ray is taken while the person evacuates into a plastic commode. A thick paste of barium is inserted into the rectum, and the person is videotaped before evacuation, while tightening the muscles, while straining and then during and after evacuation.

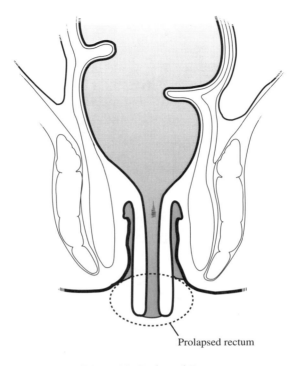

Prolapsed rectum

Figure 10: Prolapsed Rectum

The best treatment for prolapsed rectum is surgery, which requires an abdominal incision made during a stay in hospital. The surgery is not very complicated, and the results are usually very good. The rectum is pulled up and supported by a sling from the area of the backbone. In elderly or frail persons, other, less effective operations can be done via the anal canal. It is important to operate early because every time the rectum prolapses, the sphincter muscles are stretched a little more and, in time, the person will lose control.

Impaction

Impaction occurs when the stool is packed so tightly into the rectum that, with further water absorption, it dries out and blocks whatever stool forms above it. The blockage can be obscured by the passage around it of liquid stool (*overflow incontinence*), which is all that can get by. This occurs occasionally in children and is often accompanied by emotional problems. It can also occur in people whose physical movements are limited, such as someone in a wheelchair.

In impaction, the mass of impacted stool in the rectum is too large to pass. With overflow incontinence, the churning of the bowel above the blockage liquefies the stool, some of which gets by the hard stool and comes out looking like diarrhea. There is so much pressure that the watery stool may come out on its own and cause incontinence.

During a digital examination, the doctor inserts a gloved finger and can usually feel a huge dried-out mass of stool, which may be as large as a grapefruit. The inserted finger can also examine the strength of the sphincter muscles. After the doctor breaks up the stool and removes as much of it as possible, the person usually has a good bowel movement, evacuating the rest of the stool in the upper rectum. If not, a Fleet enema may be used until the rectum is clear. With normal bowel movements from a high-fibre diet, recurrence is avoided, as is the overflow incontinence.

3

Diarrhea, Gas and Other Problems

WHAT IS DIARRHEA? It's not just one loose bowel movement. Let's call significant diarrhea three watery bowel movements for more than a day. Medical attention is needed if this continues or if there is any blood. If not treated, people with severe diarrhea can go into shock and even die. Worry about diarrhea if more fluid is coming out than going in.

Our bowel movements vary not only in frequency, which is what most people talk about, but also in texture. A normally formed stool comes out and stays in the toilet in one or two large but soft pieces that do not break apart. They may float or sink depending on the gas or fat content. Slight variations in frequency or texture occur from day to day, depending on our food intake and our activity level, but the norm is up to three bowel movements a day with soft but firm stools. In diarrhea, the stool is not formed, but broken up into little pieces and accompanied by a great deal of yellow fluid. The watery consistency is the most important characteristic—especially the total volume of water passed per day.

We have all had an occasional loose bowel movement, probably related to extra garlic, spices or something else we ate the night before. This is not true diarrhea and is not a health hazard. But diarrhea that lasts longer than 2 or 3 days is significant, and the amount of fluid lost is important. Going to the toilet 15 times a day may cause so much fluid to be lost that a person becomes dehydrated. Children are especially susceptible to dehydration because of their smaller volume of body fluids; they often require emergency fluid replacement much earlier than adults—even before 3 days have passed.

Diarrhea accompanied by *abdominal cramps* may indicate food poisoning. Persistent pain or cramps, especially in only one area of the abdomen, may indicate something more serious, such as a blockage or tumour. Diarrhea accompanied by a *fever* may indicate that infection is the cause.

Bleeding may indicate something very serious, especially if it continues more than 2 or 3 days. The colour of the blood gives a good clue to the source; bright red blood comes from a fresh cut and usually means the source of the bleeding is low down. With diarrhea, however, bright red blood mixed up in the stool can also come from higher up (even as high as the stomach) because the blood moves so quickly through the bowels that it doesn't have a chance to turn dark.

Anusitis often occurs and causes bleeding when there is a lot of diarrhea. If severe, the anusitis can bleed so much that the toilet water turns all red (see Chapter 5).

Mucus is sometimes mistaken for pus, although the two are very different. Mucus is white or cream-coloured but sticky and usually seen together with stool or fluids; it is the product of an inflamed lining, like what comes out of a runny nose. *Pus* is watery and usually, seen by itself, indicates the presence of an infection; it is sometimes thicker than mucus and may be white, yellow or green. Mucus is often seen in the presence of proctitis, colitis and anusitis or anything that irritates the lining of the colon—even diarrhea if severe enough. Pus, on the other hand, is quite rare and is usually not visible with a bowel movement. In any case, pus or mucus, seen repeatedly, requires investigation by a doctor.

Diagnosing Diarrhea

The causes of diarrhea are many and varied. Medical history is important in determining the cause. Have you been to a restaurant recently, and did anyone else get sick? Have you been somewhere where you could have eaten contaminated food or water, such as South America or China? Could you have picked up a parasite? A lactose intolerance can usually be diagnosed on history alone; a blood test can be done to confirm the results of a milk-load test (see page 57), but this is usually not necessary. During a visit to the doctor, the abdomen should be examined, to make sure there are no obvious masses and to see if there is stool present that might suggest constipation or overflow incontinence. A rectal examination and sigmoidoscopy should be done, to look for any abnormality in the appearance of the lining of the rectum; this might indicate that the diarrhea is caused by ulcerative colitis or perhaps antibiotics or a parasite infestation. The stool should also be examined and cultured for parasites and bacteria.

Other investigative procedures might include colonoscopy, biopsies of the lining of the colon and, rarely, a barium enema examination.

Food poisoning, for example, is not uncommon; the most obvious clue is if the diarrhea begins 8 to 12 hours after eating tainted food at home or at a restaurant, especially if others who ate the same food or at the same restaurant are also sick.

But the most frequent cause is *anxiety*. Students often get diarrhea before writing exams, and public speakers get it before they go to the podium. However, these are specific occasions, and the diarrhea is usually mild and doesn't last long. Nervous people, especially those who hold everything inside, often have *irritable bowel syndrome*, which is characterized by abdominal complaints such as cramps, gas, constipation and diarrhea, sometimes all of them (see pages 66–68). The diarrhea is recurrent but usually not severe.

Severe diarrhea caused by stress can be difficult to treat. Sometimes, the external stimuli that cause the stressful situation can be eliminated or changed, e.g., a job or a personal conflict. However, the causes are often internally created, as in the somatizing person whose emotional problems may have physical consequences. Once the causes have been thoroughly investigated, the person may be helped by psychotherapy.

Antibiotics are a fairly frequent cause of significant and prolonged diarrhea. Antibiotics should never be prescribed for minor problems and are inappropriate for viral infections such as colds. They should only be prescribed if there is a secondary infection. Certain antibiotics, such as tetracycline and cephalosporins, kill some of the bacteria normally present in the bowel, leaving other bacteria, which then multiply quite easily and replace those killed. This imbalance causes the bowel to get irritated, creating gas, cramps and diarrhea. It can take many months for this imbalance to correct itself. In the meantime, that person will have a very touchy gut. Treatment consists of reintroducing the bacteria killed. Certain foods, such as unpasteurized yogurt and cheeses, might be increased in the diet, but they are not easy to find. An easier but more expensive way is to use supplemental capsules such as Bacid (lactobacillus), which is available without a prescription.

Diarrhea is also a symptom of *colitis*. The best-known and most frequent type is *ulcerative colitis*, in an active case of which there may be as many as 15 bowel movements a day. Bright red blood and mucus are mixed up in the stool; there might also be abdominal cramps. This continues for weeks and is most often seen in people in their twenties and thirties, although it also occurs in older people. The cause of ulcerative colitis is unknown, but recent research suggests that some genetic factors can be implicated. The condition usually affects the lower part of the colon but may spread up into the whole colon. Colitis may also be infective in origin. This diagnosis is usually made from stool cultures—growing the organism in a culture and looking for organisms under the microscope. The bacteria may have been introduced because of poor hygiene, e.g., by not washing hands thoroughly after having a bowel movement or changing a diaper. The doctor also inspects the lining of the colon—in the case of ulcerative colitis, the lining is riddled with ulcers that leak blood, mucus and pus. Treatment for colitis is a bland diet as well as thickening and slowing down the stool, accomplished with medication (such as codeine or Imodium) and long-term therapy with prescribed oral medication and suppositories.

Sensitivity to certain foods or toxins may occasionally cause diarrhea when they're ingested. The diarrhea being intermittent, it can be quite difficult to find out what a person is sensitive to. Certain substances other than lactose cause bowel upsets: spices (especially garlic), monosodium glutamate, red meat, nuts, food colouring and preservatives and toxins. Diagnosis is made by trial and error—not so easy. It is important to list all foods taken in and read labels on all prepared foods. To determine whether a suspected food is the cause, it should be eliminated from the diet for 3 days and then reintroduced to see if the symptoms recur. If no one food is suspected, then the substances mentioned above should all be eliminated from the diet and one of them reintroduced every 3 days. Allergy testing should be done next, but this is not very exact. If the diarrhea is not a reaction to a food, it may be the result of a bacterial infection. This is diagnosed in the laboratory by examining stool samples. Treatment entails preventing the reaction by avoiding the offending substance. Anti-diarrhea medication such as codeine or Imodium might also be prescribed, as might specific antibiotics in the case of a bacterial infection.

Diagnosis of a *parasite infestation* is also made from stool samples sent to the laboratory. Treatment is by the appropriate antibiotic. In most cases the person has travelled to a place such as South America, Africa, India or the Philippines where the water supply was contaminated and has ingested the parasite in contaminated water used to clean or prepare foods (e.g., salads) or drinks (e.g., ice cubes). Parasites may also be picked up from unwashed foods or from contaminated food handlers.

Coping with Diarrhea

Since diarrhea is not usually severe and goes away by itself, most often it is only necessary to slow the bowel down and thicken the stool. The following suggestions may help:

- Take a bulking agent, such as a high-fibre cereal or even Metamucil, and drink plenty of fluids.
- Change the diet to avoid anything that could irritate the bowel, such as garlic, coffee, beer, hot peppers or cola drinks.
- Use a medication, such as codeine or Imodium, to decrease the frequency of the diarrhea and the hyperactivity of the bowel.

If the diarrhea is more severe, it is important to prevent dehydration (especially in infants and the elderly). Severe and prolonged diarrhea may require hospitalization and intravenous fluids to replace the lost fluids and electrolytes, together with frequent blood analysis. Electrolyte solutions such as Gatorade may be given to children, provided there is no nausea or vomiting. Plain sugar solutions or water are not enough by themselves—they may even aggravate dehydration. Salt and electrolytes must be replaced, as they hold fluids in the body; when the electrolyte balance is upset, normal body functions are also upset. Once the diarrhea starts to settle down, the person may eat clear soups and rice, slowly adding other, easily digestible foods, such as white meat and potatoes.

Gas, Burps and Farts

Intestinal gas is one of the most frequent complaints. The build-up of gas can be so great it can make a woman look pregnant. Everyone has felt the embarrassment of making a rude smell at a social gathering or, worse, making a rude noise! Some people, particularly elderly women, may not be able to hold gas back at all, becoming so self-conscious that they won't even leave home.

"Farting," a word steeped in embarrassment, was rarely used in the past. It is still not used in "proper company" or in public. But is there any other word as descriptive or as widely understood?

Dr. Michael Levitt, a gastroenterologist from Minneapolis, Minnesota, has studied bowel gas—and gives an amusing talk on the subject of the "fragrantly flatulent." He doesn't expend a lot of hot air on such terms as gassiness or flatulence; he prefers the word "fart" to the medical term "passing flatus." I will follow Dr. Levitt's lead.

Is It Normal to Fart?

Yes. Studies have shown that most people fart an average of 13 times a day. The average daily volume of gas is 600 mL, but this varies from day to day, with a range of 200 mL to 2,000 mL. In fact, it can vary a great deal in the same person, and some people fart more than others.

One can imagine the technical difficulties of placing a sealed plastic bag over the anus to collect gas in order to measure the volume and analyze its content. Actually, the most accurate, albeit uncomfortable, way of collecting the gas is to stick tubes into the stomach, the small bowel, the colon and the rectum. The gas collected through these tubes can be kept separate from room air and analyzed in a gas chronometer. This is only a research technique—thank goodness!

Using these techniques, Dr. Michael Levitt found that farts are made up mainly of three gases, with traces of others. The main gases are hydrogen, methane and carbon dioxide. This was a startling discovery—that the gases on the inside are not the same as on the outside (the atmosphere is made up mostly of oxygen and nitrogen) or, to put it another way, that farts are quite different in composition than swallowed air. Indeed, methane and hydrogen are not present in the atmosphere in appreciable amounts. Therefore, some gas must be created in the bowel.

What Makes a Burp?

Although in some societies burping is considered a polite way of showing appreciation for a good meal, in North America it is considered very bad manners. Burping may be caused by a great deal of carbon dioxide formed in the stomach, but another cause is much more frequent—swallowed air.

Watch the throat of someone burping very carefully: the person must swallow or suck in air to have enough in the stomach to burp with. Some people learn to burp so easily that they do it subconsciously and out of habit. Burpers often excuse their actions by saying they have a "digestive problem," but it's not true. In fact, in ordinary x-rays of the upper abdomen there is only an average of about 50 mL of air in the stomach.

Burping isn't always easy: since gas rises, a person must be standing or sitting upright to burp. A person lying down can't burp because the air can't rise to the top of the stomach. In most other positions, the air will be trapped in a different part of the stomach. Therefore, to get rid of a lot of carbon dioxide after eating a fatty meal, it's best to sit or stand. After all, we burp babies in the upright position.

Causes of Intestinal Gas

Most people believe that a lot of the gas in the intestine is swallowed. People often go to great lengths to change their eating and chewing habits. They learn to eat slowly and chew well, and avoid gulping air with their food, chewing gum, using drinking straws and drinking carbonated beverages. Actually, swallowing air is a very infrequent cause of farting, although it does cause burping.

Swallowed air in the stomach is very different from the air in the rectum. However, the studies revealed that the composition of gas while it is in the stomach is almost the same as in the outside air, but something happens between the stomach and the anus to produce this very non–atmospheric gas mixture.

Further studies have shown that there are five major gases in the entire bowel: nitrogen, oxygen, carbon dioxide, hydrogen and methane. Not only do their concentrations vary from one part of the bowel to the other, but they also vary from one person to another. The concentration of nitrogen can vary from 24 to 80%, oxygen from 0.1 to 2.3%, hydrogen from 0.6 to 47%, methane from 0 to 26% and carbon dioxide from 4.3 to 29%. Hydrogen, methane and carbon dioxide comprise more than half of the bowel gas. Since these are not present in the same amounts or proportion in the atmosphere, they must be altered or made in the intestine.

The main gas in the stomach is carbon dioxide. This is produced when the hydrochloric acid produced in the stomach and ingested fatty acids react with the bicarbonate in the stomach. This occurs mostly after meals, especially fatty ones. As much as 3 L of carbon dioxide may be produced. Since carbon dioxide is not present in the colon, it must all be absorbed through the wall of the small bowel into the bloodstream.

If most people don't swallow air and if carbon dioxide is absorbed into the bloodstream, where does the gas in the colon come from? Almost all of the hydrogen and carbon dioxide are formed in the colon by bacteria.

Hydrogen and carbon dioxide are created by the action of the colonic bacteria on the remaining food matter that passes into the colon from the small bowel. Most of this matter consists of proteins, carbohydrates, sugars and fats and is already partially digested in the small bowel. It is then further broken down by the bacteria normally present in the colon. Certain elements are not broken down as well by some people as by others. As more of these foods are presented to the bacteria, more colon gas is formed. The more of these we eat, the more gas we make. The most common causes are lactose and beans.

Lactose intolerance results from an inability to break down lactose (milk sugar) into simple sugars that can be absorbed (see pages 57–59). If not broken down, lactose runs right through the gut, causing gas, bloating and diarrhea.

Beans may not be quite as dramatic a problem as lactose, but many more people have gas after eating beans. Beans contain *oligosaccharide*, a starch whose bonds are also difficult to break down in the small bowel. Again, not much of the necessary enzyme is present in the small bowel (although certain animals have lots). As in someone intolerant to lactose, the undigested element is then fermented by the colonic bacteria, which creates gas and farting. Most of us have this problem to a mild degree.

Methane differs from both hydrogen and carbon dioxide in being produced solely by the colonic bacteria; no undigested food material from the small intestine is needed to create it. It is a major constituent of the same natural gas we use in our furnaces and a component in stools that makes them float—if your stools float, then you are among the one-third of the population who have methane-producing bacteria in their intestine.

Explosive Gas Mixtures

Explosive gas mixtures are possible—we have all heard jokes about intestinal gas igniting and exploding. Methane and hydrogen may combust under certain conditions when combined with oxygen. Together with oxygen in the air, a concentration of methane from 5 to 15% and hydrogen from 4 to 74% may cause an explosion if ignited by a spark: a little explosion or one big enough to damage the colon and other, adjoining organs.

This may occur during electrocautery to remove a polyp if the bowel has not been properly prepared. Special equipment is needed to suck out the gas already in the bowel and replace it with a non-explosive gas, such as carbon dioxide, before continuing. It is important to make sure that the doctor performing this procedure has experience with the equipment, keeps a tank of carbon dioxide handy and uses it. There is no danger of this happening in colonoscopy because the laxative required for the procedure causes so much diarrhea that any explosive gases are flushed out. Also, because the person has been fasting, there should be no undigested food in the colon to be fermented by the bacteria.

Smelly farts are caused by methane or hydrogen sulphide, or both. Methane is naturally produced in the colon. Hydrogen sulphide is produced from some foods we eat.

Diagnosing Intestinal Gas

Fortunately, it's not necessary to collect gas from the rectum; diagnosis is usually made by considering diet and history. Constipation and poor bowel habits that result from not eating enough fibre or eating irregularly may also cause gas (see pages 27–36), as may tension and stress. Certain foods cause burping and farting (see below).

Foods that cause gas

- Some raw vegetables and fruits, such as apples, all types of beans (legumes), cauliflower, broccoli, turnips, onions (either raw or fried) and cabbage;
- Milk, cream, soft cheeses, ice cream and foods that include milk;
- Beer and carbonated beverages containing fructose;
- Foods containing fructose, which is not absorbed well;
- Nuts of all kinds (including coconut);
- Some baked goods such as Boston cream pie, lemon meringue pie, cherry pie and blueberry pie;
- Chocolate;
- Sweets—eating too many isn't a good idea, anyway.

How food is eaten may also cause gas and burps. Observe the throat closely as you are eating to see if any air is swallowed. Some people gulp down air with their food or as a nervous habit. Some people who chew gum and eat too fast—especially junk food grabbed on the run—also swallow air. This is the same air they breathe, though; what is not burped is absorbed into the bloodstream through the small bowel; it doesn't end up in the colon.

Much more troublesome is the gas created in the colon. A doctor should be consulted if the intestinal gas causes abdominal pain from bloating or cramps, or if there is frequent diarrhea. Medical advice can also help someone who suffers from frequent farting, especially if it is smelly. Hopefully, the offending food will be diagnosed and eliminated from the diet, solving the problem.

If the problem persists, seek medical attention. The cause may be a food sensitivity or a malabsorption problem.

Treatment of Intestinal Gas

After making sure that the bowel habits are good—there is nothing like regular bowel movements to get rid of gas, that there is no malabsorption problem and that the person is not subconsciously burping, the doctor will concentrate almost exclusively on diet as the biggest factor in causing intestinal gas. Often, the cause is *lactose intolerance*, a very clear-cut problem, easy to diagnose and fairly easy to do something about (see pages 57–59).

Beans, cauliflower and broccoli probably cause gas in more people than milk, but usually to a lesser extent. This is the category of foods that are not completely broken down into their basic elements in the small bowel. Also in this category are peas, lentils, cabbage, lettuce, onions and possibly the gluten found in wheat, corn and oats.

A product called Beano is available to help people with this problem. The tablets contain a chemical that, when taken with these foods, supplies an enzyme to partly break them down during digestion. Beano helps some people, but it must be used according to the instructions.

Other foods that may produce gas are sweeteners containing fructose (in carbonated beverages), apples, chocolate, nuts and certain berries.

Lactose Intolerance

Lactose intolerance is a frequent cause of diarrhea and may be present in a third of Asians; it is less frequent in Caucasians. After consuming something with lactose, such as milk, beer, ice cream or soft cheese, a person with lactose intolerance often has bloating, gas or diarrhea. Lactose is a long chain of simple sugars joined, or bonded together, to make up the complex sugar lactose. When we eat foods containing lactose, these bonds must be broken down by enzymes that are present in the upper small bowel. Once broken down into simple sugars, they can be absorbed through the bowel wall and into the bloodstream. It is only the simpler and short-chained sugars that are small enough to pass through the bowel wall—and be absorbed.

The enzyme needed to do this is *lactase*. In the total absence of lactase, lactose stays unchanged, attracts fluid and passes all the way through the bowel, creating lots of gas, abdominal pain and diarrhea. Those who have only a small amount of lactase will be able to break down only a small amount of lactose at a time. In other words, they can drink milk or beer very slowly without too much difficulty.

I recall the case of one man who, when asked to go on a milk diet, passed gas 70 times in one 4-hour period and a total of 141 times within 1 day. That's amazing enough; just as amazing was that he kept count each time he farted. His problem was due not to swallowing air, as other doctors had diagnosed many times before, but to a lactose intolerance. It all stopped when he eliminated lactose.

To test for a lactase deficiency, I recommend my *milk load test*. Some time when you have no gas, cramps or diarrhea, drink four glasses of milk of any kind. If within 1 hour you have gas, cramps or diarrhea, you most likely have a lactose intolerance.

The next step in diagnosing a lactose intolerance is to eliminate certain foods from the diet: milk, soft cheese, ice cream, beer, beans of all shapes and colours, whole grains, garlic, cauliflower, broccoli, turnips, parsnips and rutabaga, cabbage, apples, nuts and fatty foods.

Once the symptoms have disappeared, we reintroduce each food—starting with milk—one at a time, every 3 days to determine which is the offending food and whether there is a lactose intolerance.

Treatment consists of simply avoiding lactose-containing foods or adding the enzyme to break down the lactose before eating or drinking them.

Lactose-free milk and Lactaid (lactulose tablets put into milk to break down the lactose) are readily available. Treated milk tastes a bit sweeter and can be used for coffee, tea and cooking. Foods with lactose in them must be eliminated if the condition is severe or, if mild, reduced and taken slowly. Lactose must be broken up so that its simple sugar components can be absorbed. If lactose enters the colon, the bacteria have a field day creating gas from it.

I recommend making some dietary changes when lactose is a problem. A regular diet provides about 8 mg or less of lactose a day, primarily from milk. Lactose is also added during the processing of many foods and drug products, although its addition is not necessarily indicated on the label. However, if the label indicates the addition of milk, lactose and milk solids, the product should be avoided in severe lactase deficiency. Certain commercial preparations containing soy are available as milk substitutes, e.g., Mullsoy (Borden's) and Nutramigen (Mead Johnson).

So many foods do have milk or milk solids in them that people with a severe lactose intolerance must read the labels of prepared foods quite carefully before buying them. Lactose is also present in ice cream, beer and cheese, but only cream cheeses—older cheeses such as Cheddar and mozzarella are already partly fermented and are better tolerated.

If the diet described in the box is followed, it is important to make sure that the diet contains adequate calcium and riboflavin. Supplements may be necessary.

Foods to Avoid in Severe Lactose Intolerance

Type of Food	Foods to Avoid
Beverages	Milk, cream, buttermilk, yogurt, cereal beverages made with milk; products containing milk solids; beer
Bread and Cereal	Any baked good, breads, etc., made with cream, milk or milk solids
Cheeses	Processed and most cheeses that are not aged—especially cream cheese; commercial products containing cheese
Meat, Fish and Poultry	Any meat, fish or poultry that has been breaded or creamed; sauces, cold cuts or sausage products made with cream, milk or milk solids
Fat	Butter and margarine containing milk solids
Fruits and vegetables	Any fruit or vegetable prepared with cream, milk or milk solids
Prepared foods	Any food containing cream, milk or milk solids, such as prepared macaroni and cheese
Soup	Soups containing cream, milk or milk solids
Sweets	Milk chocolate (but pure chocolate has no lactose)
Desserts	Any dessert that contains cream, milk or milk solids, such as ice cream, sherbet and frozen yogurt

Diverticula and Diverticulitis

Diverticula is the plural of *diverticulum*, which comes from the Latin word *diverticulum*, meaning *byway*; *diverticulosis* refers to the condition of having diverticula. *Diverticulitis* is the condition of a diverticulum that becomes blocked and infected. *Diverticular disease* is a general term used to refer to the presence of diverticula and all conditions relating to them.

A diverticulum is a balloon-shaped pouch or pocket of the inner lining of the colon (see Figure 11). The pocket extends outwards through a weak spot in the wall of the colon; if large enough, it reaches right out beyond the wall. Diverticula look like a series of miniature balloons protruding out of the colon.

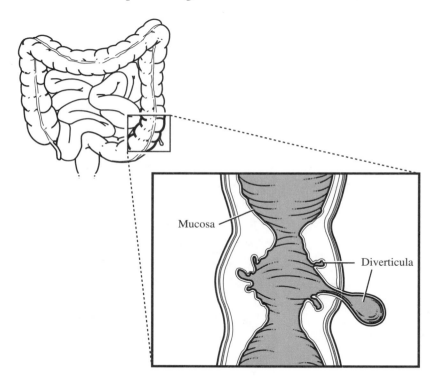

Mucosa

Diverticula

Figure 11: Diverticula

Diverticulitis is definitely a disease of 20th-century Western civilization, diverticula being rare in the populations of rural Africa and Asia. An examination of autopsies done in 1910 revealed an incidence of diverticula of only 5%; the same examination in 1980 revealed an incidence of 50%—a 10-fold increase in just 70 years, one lifetime. The number of people who died of diverticulitis, small at the beginning of this century, increased in its first half; now, however, as people begin to follow diets higher in fibre it is decreasing. An estimated 50% of people over age 50 have diverticula. In North America, 35 million people have them, and 250,000 people are admitted to hospital annually for diverticulitis at a cost of over a third of a billion dollars.

Diverticula vary in size and numbers from person to person. There may be just one diverticulum, but more often there are a few; there may even be hundreds. Most people have diverticula without knowing it. Diverticula are most numerous in the sigmoid colon, but they may extend to the entire length of the colon. Once formed, diverticula are permanent and cannot be made to disappear by conservative means. For all practical purposes, diverticula do not occur in the small bowel.

Each diverticulum has a mouth that opens into the colon. The diameter of the mouth is very important: pieces of undigested food or small, hard clumps of stool (*fecaliths*) easily enter a diverticulum with a large mouth, but they also come out again very easily; in the case of a smaller-mouthed diverticulum, that same foreign body could be pushed into the diverticulum by the pressure in the colon but would not be able to come out again.

Diverticula are associated with an increased pressure in the inner cavity (*lumen*) and located at a weak spot in the wall of the colon, where the blood vessels pass through.

Whenever there is increased pressure inside the colon, the lining (mucosa) may get pushed out through the weak areas, creating a pocket. If this pressure continues over time, the pocket enlarges and extends beyond the outer wall of the colon. The pressure is caused by constipation, an irritable bowel, straining at stool or an outflow obstruction (see appropriate sections). Hereditary factors may also play a role.

Diverticula can sometimes *bleed* from the blood vessels that lie under the lining of the colon. The blood vessel bends around the corner at the mouth of the diverticulum, where it enters the pouch. It is at that bend that bleeding sometimes occurs, because the blood vessel may get scraped or torn at that point, where it is more vulnerable. Contrary to what one would expect, bleeding usually occurs from a non-inflamed diverticulum rather than an inflamed one, perhaps because the blood vessel is more exposed. Although diverticula don't bleed very often or very much, bleeding may be a significant problem. Some diverticula bleed profusely, requiring a transfusion and emergency surgery.

Sometimes people with diverticula get *abdominal cramps*, set off by small seeds and bits of nuts, which may be hard and sharp, getting stuck. Cramps are most common in a diverticulum with a small mouth. The colon contracts its muscle in the area of the diverticulum to try to push out the contents of the diverticulum. Since the diverticulum has no muscle of its own, it cannot push itself; the diverticulum can only empty as the result of the churning of the colon. This is inefficient and sometimes ineffective. The cramps are usually in the left lower quadrant of the abdomen and tend to be intermittent. About three-quarters of people with diverticula have these pains and often mistake them for constipation.

About one-quarter of people with diverticula also have a history of *constipation*. Another quarter complain of *diarrhea,* which results from the irritated bowel's attempts to empty out the diverticulum. *Bowel spasms* are also often present.

What is Diverticulitis?

Diverticulitis is a term many people are more familiar with than diverticula. It is a condition where diverticula are clogged and infected, and is associated with a higher incidence of gallstones, varicose veins, ischemic heart disease, hiatus hernia, hemorrhoids and possibly appendicitis. These are all rare in the populations of rural Africa (so is colon cancer); their diet is generally high in fibre and low in fat, and they have good bowel habits. Incidence of diverticular disease and colon cancer is also very low in Japan, although when Japanese people change their diet to a more Western one, the incidence of both increases dramatically.

Diverticulitis occurs in about 17% of people with diverticula. A second attack occurs in only a third of these people, usually within the first 5 years. In most cases, diverticulitis is caused by a hard stool or by something with hard, jagged edges, such as nuts or seeds, getting caught in a small-mouth diverticulum. If the churning of the bowel can't empty it out in time, the diverticulum is irritated and may then become infected.

Diverticulitis has most of the symptoms of a blocked diverticulum, as well as those caused by the abscess. However, the hallmarks are a *fever* (above 100°F or 38°C) and an *increase in the number of white blood cells* (indicated by a blood test). The *abdominal pains* are more severe and continuous rather than intermittent, and usually the left lower quadrant of the abdomen is tender to the touch. In advanced cases, a mass resulting from a walled-off abscess can be felt in that spot.

The abscess is the result of an infection; it may grow and break open (perforate). A *perforated diverticulum* is a serious, life-threatening situation. Usually the pus, bacteria and stool remain in the same area and become sealed off from the rest of the abdomen. Occasionally, the pus and the contents of the bowel flow freely and spread into the abdominal cavity, causing widespread *peritonitis*, which is extremely dangerous. In either case, emergency surgery is required to stop the leak and clean out the infective debris.

Recurrent mild diverticulitis is more frequent than perforation. It causes the formation of fibrous scar tissue laid down around the diverticulum and the adjacent colon. This scarring may narrow the diameter of the bowel and make it stiffer; the more the narrowing, the harder it is for the stool to pass. This results in cramps, usually in the left side of the abdomen, that become more frequent and severe with each attack. If the narrowing progresses, blockage may occur. This requires urgent surgery, although the condition is not as serious as a perforation because there is no associated infection.

Diagnosis of Diverticular Disease

Ordinary diverticula are usually discovered during a colonoscopy or barium enema x-ray done for some other reason. The doctor, suspecting diverticular disease, will take a thorough medical history, including a history of any abdominal pain, cramps (intermittent or constant) and bowel habits. An abdominal examination will check for tenderness or swelling in the lower left part of the abdomen. If suspecting diverticulitis, the doctor will take the person's temperature, test the blood and possibly do an ultrasound. After the diverticulitis has settled down, the doctor might do further tests.

A *barium enema x-ray* should never be done if diverticulitis or perforation is suspected. The barium could leak through the open diverticulum into the abdominal cavity, doing severe damage. However, a barium enema x-ray is helpful for diagnosing diverticular disease (one of the few reasons justifying this procedure). On the x-ray, the barium reveals little white pockets that extend beyond the edge of the colon—a characteristic of diverticulosis. If any abnormality is found, a colonoscopy may be called for.

Colonoscopy also shows diverticula but, like the barium enema x-ray, should be avoided if the person has had diverticulitis recently. However, it has two advantages over x-ray: there is no radiation, and the diverticula can be directly checked for signs of inflammation. The pockets can be examined, and it is easy to see if they have small or large mouths. It is not so easy to see an infected pocket. Sometimes, despite the laxatives taken to clean out the bowel before a colonoscopy, small bits of stool can be seen stuck in the diverticula. Colonoscopy should always be done prior to elective surgery for diverticular disease, to rule out the presence of other lesions, especially polyps or cancers, in the rest of the colon. Also, small growths that might be in the same area as the diverticula are easier to see than on an x-ray (which is distorted by the diverticula). I have removed polyps in a number of people with diverticular disease because I found growths during the colonoscopy that were not visible on a barium x-ray.

Treatment for Diverticular Disease

A hundred years ago, our ancestors probably didn't have diverticula. Why not? Diet! Even today, most people do not need further treatment as long as they change their diet. If they *increase the amount of the insoluble fibre and water* in their diet they will have large, soft bowel movements 1 to 3 times daily (see pages 32–33). Preventing constipation and not straining at stool makes it unlikely that the diverticula will increase in size or number and helps avoid complications.

If the diverticula cause cramps in the left lower part of the abdomen, even with good bowel movements, the person should *avoid eating nuts and especially seeds* such as sesame, poppy and caraway. These are most likely getting caught in the diverticula and causing the pain.

Diverticulitis should always be treated by a doctor. *Mild diverticulitis* may be treated without surgery, usually with a fluid or soft diet free of seeds and nuts along with a course of antibiotics. After the condition has improved, a high-fibre diet (without seeds!) should be followed to prevent recurrence. In the past, it was common to treat diverticulitis by prescribing a low-fibre diet that would put the bowel "at rest," but this has been proven ineffective. However, it is now recommended that those with a history of significant diverticulosis avoid eating nuts and large seeds.

Those with a history of *severe or recurrent diverticulitis* should make sure their diets include 50 g of fibre a day; even the seeds in cucumbers, tomatoes, strawberries, raspberries, certain breads and so on should be avoided. Severe diverticulitis requires treatment in hospital with intravenous feeding, antibiotics and bed rest. This helps rest the bowel so that the inflammation can settle down. Surgery is required in fewer than 20% of people with severe diverticulitis—that means at least 80% leave the hospital greatly improved without surgery.

However, if surgery is required, the affected part of the bowel (usually the sigmoid colon) is removed and the two ends joined together. (This is called *surgical resection* and is usually recommended after the third severe attack.) In some cases of perforated diverticulitis, the part of the colon that is above the affected area must be extended through the abdominal wall; this creates a *colostomy*—an opening where the stool can be collected into a bag. The colostomy prevents the contents of the colon from getting into the area of the surgery so it can heal without risk of contamination by the bowel contents. When healing is complete, the colostomy can usually be closed, resulting in normal bowel movements again.

In recent years, the need for surgery has decreased because of better antibiotics and improved drainage techniques. A drainage tube can be guided by CAT scan into the abscess to drain it, which may make an operation unnecessary. Diet, too, has decreased the chance of further attacks. One study followed a hundred people with diverticulitis, severe enough to be treated in hospital, for 5 years; 90% of those on a high-fibre diet had no recurrences.

Irritable Bowel Syndrome

Irritable bowel syndrome (IBS) is probably the commonest problem seen by bowel specialists—some say up to 60% of their patients have an irritable bowel. It is characterized by little cramps, usually in different locations of the small and large bowel. They act like involuntary mini-blockages and are accompanied by *abdominal cramps*, *constipation* and *gas*. Sometimes there is also diarrhea, which may be followed by relief.

IBS varies in degree from mild to very severe and incapacitating and should be thoroughly investigated to rule out any other bowel problems. It is a diagnosis based on exclusion. It can be very difficult to diagnose because there is no lesion to be found, although the symptoms are real. People sometimes go to several doctors before they accept this diagnosis because it is hard for them to understand that anxiety can produce such severe and uncomfortable symptoms.

Emotions have an important role in the function of the bowels. For example, a woman who was a somatizer—a person with a physical complaint caused by an emotional problem—was separated from her husband. She had severe abdominal pain and some diarrhea; as soon as her divorce was over, the diarrhea and pain cleared up on their own.

Another example: a 45-year-old man had a 4-year history of very severe rectal pains. He was so sensitive that whenever a bit of stool entered the rectum, he had to either have a bowel movement or give himself an enema to get the stool out. He complained of having "diarrhea," because of the fullness and urge to go so often, but this was not true diarrhea. It turned out that he had lost his job 4 years earlier, just before the rectal pain started, and he was still unemployed. With the assistance of psychotherapy, he was able to deal with his emotional problem, thus clearing up the physical problem.

IBS is best described as a *motility disorder* of the bowel. Instead of the bowel cramping or contracting along its length to propel its contents forward, it cramps irregularly. Characteristically, the pain moves around to different parts of the bowel and abdomen at different times, trapping gas and stool in different areas of the bowel. The gas and stool can move neither up nor down. The cramps are probably more uncomfortable when they are in the colon because there is increased pressure on the wall of the colon due to the stool present. The most frequent site of this pain is in the lower left part of the abdomen. The contents churn and the bowel bloats in between the two areas of spasm, causing pain and swelling. In severe cases, the whole abdomen may be so distended the person looks pregnant.

Treatment of Irritable Bowel Syndrome

IBS is treated by learning how to *manage anxiety and stress*. This can be hard, particularly for those who are good at concealing their levels of anxiety. Learning stress management methods and relaxation techniques may reduce the anxiety causing IBS; this may require a complete change of lifestyle. In some cases, psychotherapy is effective.

Medications such as Colpermin, coated peppermint oil capsules or pinaverium bromide tablets deal, at best, only with the symptoms and are therefore not very helpful. Surgery is not advised because it cannot treat the actual cause.

Following a diet high in fibre and drinking plenty of water reduces the pressure in the colon, of benefit to people with IBS, especially those whose condition is in the colon (ICS). Does increased bulk in stools help them? According to a recent study, pressure in the colon of a group following a high-fibre diet returned to normal within 6 months. This is strong evidence in favour of a high-fibre diet, because it adds bulk that stretches the spasms. As with diverticular disease, the days of recommending a low-fibre diet are long gone.

4

Piles—Hemorrhoids

Myths and Misconceptions

M Y HEMORROIDS are killing me."
"I have a big, painful hemorrhoid."
"My itching is from hemorrhoids."
"My hemorrhoids bother me two or three times a year."
"I got hemorrhoids from sitting on a cold surface."
"My hemorrhoid problem started with my last pregnancy."

Most people believe anal pain and bleeding are caused by hemor-rhoids. But anal pain is almost never due to hemorrhoids, and bleed-ing is more often due to something else. In fact, many people who didn't have them have been operated on for hemorrhoids. Hemor-rhoids are unjustly blamed for most problems in the anal area. But lots of other things can go wrong there, too. The information in this chapter will help you distinguish what's myth from what's truth. You will learn what a hemorrhoid is and what causes it, so you can decide what medical care you need.

Hemorrhoid and pile mean the same thing. Hemorrhoid comes from the Latin word for bleeding. Pile comes from the Greek word for protrusion or swelling. Since all symptomatic hemorrhoids pro-trude but not all bleed, I use the term pile. It's also simpler and easier to spell, an added bonus.

What is a Pile?

A pile is a swelling or protrusion with a core of loose tissue containing a lot of blood vessels. It is covered by the lining of the anal canal (mucosa) and is attached to the side wall of the upper end of the anal canal above the dentate line (see Figure 12). A pile is not located in the centre of the anal canal, as so many people believe, but it protrudes (sticks out) into the space or canal.

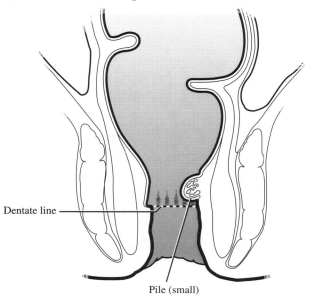

Dentate line

Pile (small)

Figure 12: Pile or Hemorrhoid

A pile can range from small to large. If it is small, you don't know it is there; many people have small piles that are of no consequence. If it is a little larger, it will protrude down the anal canal and you may notice a feeling of fullness. A large pile comes out of the anal opening during a bowel movement and is more likely to bleed. This is what usually bothers someone enough to seek medical attention. Something is clearly not quite right.

Most protruding (or prolapsing) piles will go back in by themselves but then come right out again with the next bowel movement or after heavy lifting. It isn't commonly known that a protruding pile is usually easy to push back up inside. This doesn't hurt and gives instant relief. In time, though, a pile can get too big to push back easily, so it stays out.

When piles are outside they may bleed and leak a smelly discharge that stains the underwear. Piles do not bleed very often or very much until they are big enough to protrude. In fact, some people's frustrated attempts to get the stains out are what finally send them to the doctor!

There are three main or *primary* sites for piles, one on the right side of the anal canal above the dentate line and two on the left. Imagine that noon is at the backbone: the primary piles are at 3, 7 and 11 o'clock. Then there may be three more smaller *secondary* piles in between the primary ones. It's often hard to know how many piles there are because large ones may hide smaller ones. There is rarely only one pile—the average is four.

One of the biggest mistakes people make is to call any swelling on the outside skin a hemorrhoid or pile. Don't forget, a pile is attached to the lining of the anal canal above the dentate line. The term "external pile," sometimes used, is inaccurate.

Piles are not painful. This is because they are covered by *mucosa*, the mucous membrane that lines the entire bowel from mouth right down to the dentate line. Mucosa contains no pain nerves. Pain nerves are only present in the skin which starts below the dentate line—below the piles. Pain is felt if the skin below the dentate line is pinched. No pain is felt if the mucosa is pinched. This fundamental point explains why the new methods of treating piles work so well. The conventional hemorrhoidectomy in hospital (an operation in which part of the skin is cut away), never required, causes unnecessary pain.

Causes of Piles

Piles begin as small bits of loose lining on the side wall of the anal canal. In time, they enlarge and bulge into the opening of the canal (*lumen*).

The main cause of piles is probably bearing down, or *straining*, on the toilet. The more you strain, the larger the piles become and the

more they protrude. They occur frequently, for instance, in a constipated person who strains at stool. Even those people who are not
constipated but consider the toilet seat their throne, where they can
sit in peace and quiet for half an hour, are very likely to get piles—a
little-known fact. I can often tell that someone has been sitting too
long on the throne! This loose lining being the forerunner of piles, I
recommend that no one spend more time than necessary on the toilet—2 minutes is usually long enough—unless the lid is closed!

The most frequent cause of straining, *constipation*, is usually con-
trolled with high-fibre diets and water, so this cause of piles can almost be discounted (see pages 27–36).

It is amusing to hear all the myths about piles, many of them still
believed. Those who spend a lot of time driving, such as truckers and
taxi drivers, claim piles as their disease; many think that pregnancy or
sitting on a cold wet surface causes them. None of this is true. Piles
come from straining, with a little bit of help, possibly, from weak
supporting tissue of the anal canal, a condition which may be genetic. Piles do seem to be a family characteristic—but so are constipation and straining at stool and sitting too long on the toilet. I
suspect that it has more to do with parental examples: kids often
learn from their parents to eat junk foods and to avoid both eating
fibre and drinking water—hence, constipation may be learned, not
inherited. The bad habit of sitting too long on the toilet children also
copy from their parents. In fact, I know of at least two lawyers who
read their legal documents while sitting on the toilet in their law office: they claimed it was the only place they wouldn't be interrupted.
Sitting too long on the toilet, straining and constipation are much
more important factors in the cause of piles.

Symptoms of Piles

So many things may be confused with piles that it is important to
have a clear understanding of the symptoms. Different symptoms
suggest a different diagnosis, which require a different treatment.

Some symptoms are unique to piles, while others have many causes. It is very important to have a doctor check them early, because early diagnosis means early treatment, which may prevent serious complications later on.

One obvious indication of piles is the presence of two or three soft, rounded, painless *masses*. These bumps usually stick out after a bowel movement or after straining to reach something high or to lift something heavy. Straining makes the piles fill with blood, so sometimes they collapse or become smaller in between bowel movements and go back up inside until the next bowel movement. There are usually at least two, and they can be pushed back up into the anal canal, where they usually stay until the next bowel movement. Most people don't know they can do this and so don't try. If the problem recurs only a few times a year or only during pregnancy, it is not due to piles. Piles typically occur, at first, only with straining from constipation and, later, with most or all bowel movements. Smaller piles don't protrude, so they can be hard to diagnose, although diagnosis is made easier if the person strains during the exam.

However, these lumps may be due to something else. Swelling at the anal opening may be caused by a polyp, which may protrude but almost always occurs singly and doesn't squirt blood. It is also relatively painless. Or the lump may be a hematoma (blood clot), which is painful and can't be pushed back up inside (see page 110).

Another clear diagnostic indication of piles is bright red *blood* that squirts into the toilet bowl during a bowel movement. It actually squirts in time with the heart beat and continues until the pile is replaced. This rhythmic squirting is unique to protruding piles (smaller piles don't bleed this way), but there may also be blood that drips into the toilet or is wiped onto the toilet paper. Sometimes, enough blood is lost to cause a feeling of tiredness, especially in women who are menstruating; in rare instances, a blood transfusion is required. Anusitis causes bleeding more often than piles do (see Chapter 6).

Piles are usually *painless*. Thus, pain may indicate something other than piles, most often hematoma.

Smaller piles that do not protrude sometimes give one the sensation of needing to have a bowel movement, causing a *feeling of fullness* or *non-completion* (i.e., feeling as though evacuation is not finished). However, this sensation is more often caused by irritation of the mucosa (lining) than by piles.

A watery mucus *discharge* may occur if a pile is so big that it protrudes into the anal canal part way or completely, especially if it stays out; this discharge can irritate the skin around the anus. However, this discharge and the skin irritation are more frequently caused by anusitis.

Because piles are so frequently confused with other conditions or are misdiagnosed, I analyzed a consecutive series of 100 people who had been referred to the Rudd Clinic by their family doctors for treatment for piles. It would not be unreasonable to assume, therefore, that most of these people had piles. But when the results were tabulated, I found that only 31% had piles as the main diagnosis; the other 69% had something else; 37% of the total studied had anusitis. This is a good illustration of how often anorectal problems are blamed on piles.

Symptoms of Piles

The following are the most common symptoms of piles, starting with the most important:

- *Soft, round masses* that protrude after a bowel movement and can be completely replaced into the anal canal;
- *Bright red blood* that squirts into the toilet after a bowel movement or sometimes drips into the toilet or is wiped on the toilet paper when the pile is protruding;
- *Little or no pain;*
- *Feeling of fullness or non-completion;*
- Watery mucus *discharge.*

Diagnosing Piles

If it isn't broken, don't fix it—if the piles cause no discomfort, there is no need for immediate treatment. In fact, many people have small piles and don't even know they're there. But if the piles prolapse or bleed, or if there is a feeling of fullness or non-completion or a discharge, they should be treated.

The first thing the doctor will do is *ask a few questions* about when the bumps appear and whether they bleed or are painful. It is always a good idea to be prepared for this conversation, especially because thinking about the matter beforehand makes it less uncomfortable to talk about.

Questions to Consider

- Are there protrusions that come out with a bowel movement?
- Does this occur regularly or is it just once or twice a year?
- Can you push the protrusions back in completely?
- How many are there?
- Do they squirt or drip blood into the toilet?
- Are they painful?

Then the doctor will do a *visual examination* of the anal area. Because it is sometimes difficult to see this area, you can help by holding your buttocks apart. This may expose a small pile that might otherwise be missed. The doctor will also do a *digital examination* to feel for swellings.

The diagnosis should be confirmed by using an *anoscope* to see the piles. You might be asked to strain, to push the piles down so they can be seen more easily, since piles may collapse when they are not filled with blood and especially if you are in the "bottoms-up" position. A *sigmoidoscopy* is necessary and a *colonoscopy* advisable (see pages 10–11 and 13–17), in people age 45 or older, to rule out any other causes, which is particularly important if there is any blood.

Treatment of Piles

Any piles that bleed heavily should be treated immediately. A medium-sized pile that does not protrude or squirt blood does not require treatment. Instead, it is more effective to fix the cause—constipation or straining at stool or sitting too long on the toilet (see pages 27–36). Any accompanying anusitis should be treated, as it is usually the cause of any bleeding other than squirting blood (see Chapter 5). If the condition doesn't improve or the piles get bigger, other forms of treatment should be applied.

Ointments, creams and suppositories are heavily promoted for the treatment of piles. This billion-dollar industry manufactures products such as Preparation H, Anusol or Proctocedyl. But without a proper diagnosis, a person might be using these and not even have piles. Furthermore, the products don't treat piles so much as they relieve other conditions, such as itching or pain. Yet itching, pain and bleeding are more often the result of anusitis (see Chapter 6). Therefore, I do not recommend using these products for the treatment of piles.

The most effective treatment of piles is to combine *ligation and cryotherapy*. We have used this method at the Rudd Clinic since 1972 with excellent results. Banding, or ligation, of piles by itself is a very simple method, coincidentally one of the first ever used. The modern method, introduced by Dr. F. Salmon, was perfected by Dr. James Barron in 1963. Now the more frequently used treatment than the operation performed in hospitals in North America, it is being more widely adopted in Europe, encouraged, I hope, in some small part by the teaching and writing done by the physicians at the Rudd Clinic. We have developed an instrument that makes this method almost painless and the whole procedure takes only a minute or two. Normal activities are not interrupted, although lifting heavy objects and standing or walking for extended periods should be avoided for 2 to 3 days.

Ligation, or *banding*, uses a ligator, a special instrument loaded with a very small elastic band (see Figure 13). Looking through the anoscope, the doctor uses forceps to pull the pile through the metal ring holding the band. The band is then pushed off the ligator onto the "neck" of the pile. Some people find the sound of the band coming off unsettling, but the process is painless. I always say something at that time. The elastic band must be placed precisely so that it encompasses the entire pile; otherwise, a tag or edge remains and another treatment is required at the same location. Once the supply of blood to the pile is cut off, the pile dies. The band is left in place and falls away into the toilet at the same time as the pile dissolves or melts away; this occurs over the next 3 to 12 days (the older the person, the longer it takes). It is hard to tell when this happens—the only sign may be a drop of blood at the time of separation. People often have to be assured it has actually fallen off.

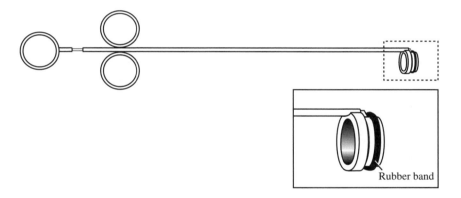

Figure 13: The Rudd Clinic Ligator

Cryotherapy (the application of extreme cold) for piles was introduced by Dr. Martin Lewis in 1969. With a metal probe cooled by liquid nitrogen, extreme cold is applied to the pile, causing the water in the cells to freeze. The pile is killed by the cold. If cryotherapy is used on its own, the pile dies and dissolves over the next 10 days (just like a frostbitten toe). As it dissolves, it leaks an irritating and smelly discharge. Also, using cryotherapy to treat a large prolapsed pile or applying it to healthy skin causes pain. If more than one pile is treated at a time, the resulting swelling may block the passage of stool.

The combination of cryotherapy and ligation allows the band to be removed immediately. The band separates the pile from the normal tissue, making the abnormal tissue easier to treat with cryotherapy. The band stops the warm blood from flowing through the pile, making the freezing more effective. And we can use nitrous oxide, which is not as cold as liquid nitrogen and much easier and cheaper to use. Because it takes place above the dentate line, where there are no pain nerves, the process is painless. The two procedures only take 2 minutes, unlike other treatments, which may require hospitalization and long recovery times.

Fewer than 1% of people treated with ligation and cryosurgery have any significant bleeding. Fewer than 3% have any significant pain, almost always from a blood clot caused by walking too much, eating spicy or irritating foods, or lifting heavy objects—these activities should be avoided for the first 2 days after the procedure—or by straining at stool.

One or, occasionally, two piles are treated at a time. Treating more increases discomfort. Usually two follow-up visits, about 2 weeks apart, to the doctor will complete the treatment. A final exam 6 months later is recommended. At this time, if there are any secondary piles or loose lining, the person has likely been constipated and straining at stool or sitting too long on the toilet. This loose lining is a forerunner of piles; correcting constipation and bad bowel habits will prevent a recurrence. Very few people have a recurrence of piles after ligation and cryotherapy if they are not constipated or do not strain at stool.

Using ligation and cryotherapy together means the person experiences even less discomfort. When ligation is used on its own, the O-ring must be left in place to prevent blood from flowing into the pile so that the tissue will die and dissolve on its own. This sometimes causes some discomfort—an aching feeling or fullness for the first 2 or 3 days. This discomfort is avoided by the use of cryotherapy because the band is divided after the cryotherapy is applied. Also, when the band is left in place, each pile has to be treated one at a time with a 2-week gap between treatments; using cryotherapy and dividing the band may allow two piles to be treated simultaneously, which is more convenient for the person if travel is involved and reduces the risk of bleeding caused by a band left in place: as the pile dissolves, the band might tug at the lining or the edge of the pile and cause bleeding.

Unlike a conventional hemorrhoidectomy, the combination of ligation and cryotherapy is a very cost-effective way to treat piles. It has a high success rate and does not require any hospitalization or anesthesia; nor does it normally require any significant time away from modified activities. This does not even take into account the priceless benefits of reduced risk in comparison with general anesthesia and avoidance of any significant pain or anxiety. The procedure saves government and insurers millions of dollars—indeed, in some places in the United States, health insurance no longer covers a hemorrhoidectomy.

Over the century, many different methods have been tried for treating piles, championed by one doctor or another as the best, only to be discarded. Such will be the fate of the hemorrhoidectomy, which is on the decline right now. Unfortunately, it is still occasionally used.

A *hemorrhoidectomy* is an operation to cut out the piles and the skin outside them. It must be done in hospital, usually under general anesthesia. Because some skin is removed, the area is usually quite painful for 2 to 3 weeks. Several modifications have been made to this technique in an effort to decrease the post-operative pain. One is to close the skin edges at the end of the operation. Another is to use a laser instead of a knife to cut the skin away (*laser hemorrhoidectomy*); the laser cuts the tissue by applying a beam of light that creates heat. The beam cuts just like a conventional knife, so it is the same operation using a different and much more expensive tool to cut the pile away. The laser cannot cut through a large mass of tissue quickly, although it does control bleeding well. There is the same amount of pain after the operation.

None of these techniques helps decrease the pain significantly. Moreover, complications may occur after surgery. There is the risk of infection and bleeding, and any formation of scar tissue during the healing process may narrow the anal canal, causing anal stenosis (see pages 37–38). Because of the pain and risk of complications, not to mention the expense of a hospital stay and 3 weeks' recovery time off work, I never recommend hemorrhoidectomy as an effective or efficient way to treat piles, even large piles. Some doctors claim that banding can't be done on large piles, but this is untrue. I have not done a hemorrhoidectomy for 25 years.

Another method accompanied by risk is *dilatation*. Developed by the British surgeon Dr. Peter Lord, this method is based on the assumption that most people with piles also have a narrowed anal opening, so they strain at stool, which causes the piles. Dilation breaks down the "narrowed ring" of the anal opening, stretching it to the width of eight fingers. The procedure requires a general anesthetic in hospital. Because dilation may result in the loss of sphincter control, it is not recommended, either. Furthermore, I do not see this narrowed ring in many people with piles.

One recent technique is to use an *infrared beam* to injure the blood vessels beneath the lining of the pile that supply it with blood. This causes clots to form that close off the supply of blood; without blood, the pile dissolves. This treatment can be done in the doctor's office. Although this method can work well on small piles, I have found that it causes pain and isn't very effective on larger ones.

Another recent method is to use *electrical current* to kill the pile. An electric current is passed between two probes, killing the pile. It too is painful, although it can work well on small and medium-sized piles. The treatment requires expensive equipment and so is unlikely to become popular as an office treatment.

Benefits of Ligation and Cryosurgery

In my experience, no treatment for piles is as effective as the combination of ligation and cryosurgery. In fact, it is the procedure most doctors prefer to have done on themselves. With this technique, the recurrence rate of piles is usually only about 5%, which is just as good as, if not better than, the conventional hemorrhoidectomy but without the disadvantages and expense of invasive surgery. However, the recurrence rate is very difficult to assess because it depends so much on individual bowel habits. If someone were to come back 5 years later complaining of piles, unless they had been straining a lot at stool or sitting too long on the toilet, anusitis (see Chapter 6) or a hematoma (see pages 110–114) is more likely.

The money saved in avoiding hospitalization, anesthetic and medications, not to mention time away from regular activities, for the 40,000 people who have been treated at the Rudd Clinic adds up to over $150 million. It's impossible to put a price on the cost of pain, the risk of an anesthetic and the anxiety of going into hospital. So clearly this method benefits all involved, including governments and health insurers, which will save millions of taxpayers' money.

Ligation and Cryosurgery versus Hemorrhoidectomy[a]

	Hemorrhoidectomy *(hospital)*	*Ligation and Cryosurgery* *(office)*
Doctor's fees	$650	$265[b]
Assistant	$175	Not applicable
Anesthetist	$200	Not applicable
Hospital stay ($800/day x 4)	$3,200	$0
Time off work	?	$0
Total cost	$4,225	$265

[a] Amounts vary in different areas.

[b] This amount is based on the initial consultation and treatment at a cost of $85 plus $60 each for three subsequent treatments.

5

Rectal Bleeding

N OTHING strikes fear in the hearts of men and women more than blood coming from the rectum. Fortunately, "rectal" bleeding is not often serious. The cause is usually quite simple. However, having said that, I must add that bleeding is the most frequent sign of bowel cancer and should always be thoroughly checked out by a doctor.

The term "rectal bleeding" is inaccurate because the blood comes much more often from the anal canal than from the rectum. Occasionally, it comes from the colon (above the rectum). But most people use the term rectal bleeding to refer to any blood from the anal area.

It's often easy to guess where the bleeding is coming from once you know the clues. You might even have an idea as to the cause. But you can never be certain until you have consulted your doctor.

Colour of the Blood

The colour of the blood is a good clue as to whether it's coming from low down in the bowel (anal canal or rectum), higher up in the colon, or even the stomach (ulcer).

First, what colour is blood normally? Let's call the colour of the blood when you cut yourself bright red. It is bright red because it is arterial blood and has just come from the lungs, where it was freshly oxygenated. Once blood leaves the artery and is exposed to the air, it turns darker red. This is because the oxygen comes out of the blood. The longer the blood has been out in the air, whether it is inside the bowel or not, the darker it gets.

If the blood is *bright red*, it is coming from low down—most likely the anal canal or rectum. If the source of the bleeding is higher up in the colon, by the time it gets down to the rectum and out with a bowel movement, it has turned *dark red*. If it has come from the stomach and is not associated with diarrhea, the blood is truly black and very smelly—this is called *melena*. The blood from the stomach is black because of the action of the stomach acid on it. In the case of diarrhea, stool moves through the bowels too quickly for the blood to darken. The opposite is true for constipation.

Sometimes the blood comes out in *clots*, which people sometimes describe as "bits of flesh." It takes time for blood to clot; to do so, it must stay still in a puddle while it forms. If it is a dark red clot, it probably comes from higher up. If the clot is brighter, it is from the lower colon but not the anal canal.

Sometimes, the blood first appears bright red but, an hour or two later, is darker or in clots. This means that the bleeding is slowing down or has stopped. It takes a while for the blood to be evacuated in the stool.

Location of the Blood

The key question is: Is the blood on the toilet paper, on underwear, in the toilet water, on the surface of the stool or mixed up inside the stool?

Bright red blood seen only on the toilet paper, although it can be quite alarming, is a frequent occurrence; most of us experience it at one time or another. The blood usually comes from the irritated lining of the anal canal, the surrounding skin, or both. It is rarely serious.

Where Does That Blood Come From?

Colour and location of blood	Probable source
Bright red blood	
• on the toilet paper	Irritation in the anal canal or prolapsing pile
• in the toilet water	Inflammation in the anal canal; inflammation or cancer in the rectum or lower colon
• squirting into toilet	Prolapsing pile
Streak	
• bright red on surface of stool	Fissure (anal canal) or rectal polyp
• dark red on surface of stool	Polyp in sigmoid colon or diverticulum
Dark red blood	
• in the water (small amount)	Cancer or inflammation in the rectum or sigmoid colon
• mixed in with stool	Cancer or inflammation higher up in the colon

If the blood is in the toilet, it's important to determine whether it is dripping or squirting into the water or whether it comes with the stool. Blood *dripping* into the toilet usually comes from a smaller surface vessel which has been scraped by a stool as it goes by, especially if the stool is hard. If the blood is bright red, the bleeding site is most likely in the anal canal. Blood *squirting* into the toilet is almost always from a protruding pile (see Chapter 4).

A *streak* of blood on the surface of the stool comes from a small raw spot, a polyp or tumour which bleeds as the stool passes it. If the blood is *on the surface* of the stool, the blood source is probably low down in the colon or rectum because the blood was added to the outside of the stool after it had already been formed.

However, if the blood is *mixed in* with the stool, the source is higher up in the colon since the bleeding occurred where the stool was still soft and still in the process of solidifying. The only variations occur whenever the stool is moving faster or slower than normal.

Paying attention to these kinds of details helps the doctor make a more accurate diagnosis. That's why it's helpful to be prepared beforehand.

Causes of Rectal Bleeding

Bleeding occurs in two main situations: first, when the lining of the bowel is irritated and damaged; and second, when there is a growth.

Inflamed and irritated tissue looks redder than normal because more blood is flowing through the tissues and more blood vessels have opened up to carry it. It's a very sensitive part of the anatomy, so if you rub it hard enough, it becomes irritated and turns red. Thin skin and mucosa are easily inflamed. Thick skin, like the skin on the sole of the foot, is not. Severely inflamed thin tissue (like the anal canal) readily develops breaks in its surface which bleed easily, especially when the raw area is scraped by a hard stool.

Anusitis is the most frequent cause of rectal bleeding, although not many people use this term to describe it. The blood is bright red and usually seen on the toilet paper. It is the result of anal irritation; there is no associated swelling. Anusitis can cause a large amount of bleeding (see Chapter 6).

Piles or hemorrhoids may bleed, although the bleeding is usually from the inflamed lining of the anal canal over the pile—anusitis—and not the pile itself. Bleeding that squirts or pumps a fine stream of bright red blood into the toilet water is characteristic of piles. The blood comes from an artery pumping in time with the heart beat. This occurs because the sphincter muscle clamps down enough on the upper part of the pile to hinder the blood's return to the heart, but not enough to stop the arterial blood pumped by the heart to the pile, which is at a higher pressure (see Chapter 4).

An *anal fissure* is a cut or tear in the lower anal canal, typically resulting in a tearing pain during a bowel movement followed by relief for a while and then ending with a burning stinging pain about half an hour later. The raw cut or wound when scraped or stretched will bleed. This also results in a streak or fine line of blood on the outer surface of the formed stool (see pages 99–105).

A painful swelling which suddenly bursts and bleeds is usually a *hematoma* (blood clot). This release of blood typically results in immediate relief of the pain. The bleeding persists for a few days and becomes darker as it slows down and sometimes clots (see pages 110–115).

A *polyp* bleeds even less. On the infrequent occasion a polyp bleeds, the blood usually comes from one spot, leaving a characteristic fine line or streak of blood on the surface of the stool. Since polyps bleed so rarely, they rarely give any indication of their presence, and it's hard to know they're there (see pages 132–134).

Bleeding can also come from the surface of a *tumour*—especially if it is ulcerated. This is typical of a cancerous tumour, where the surface cells of the tumour die and leave a raw area, which bleeds. In someone with *colon cancer*, especially a small tumour, there may be no blood or only occasionally (e.g., not every day), or there might be so little blood that it can't be detected with the naked eye. This is why it is so important to have an examination even if you see blood only once. The earlier the source is diagnosed, the sooner treatment can begin. This is also why screening tests take samples for blood for several days; testing several samples reduces the possibility of a false negative that would give a false sense of security. It cannot be stressed enough: blood on even one occasion must be investigated.

Irritated lining does occur higher up in the rectum and colon. This is called *proctitis* (in the rectum) or *colitis* (in the colon). It is most often seen in ulcerative colitis, which is relatively uncommon. In this condition, the blood may be mixed in with the stool. The presence of irritation does not automatically mean there is an infection. Even when there is some infection, if it is on the surface, it drains freely. An infection or *abscess* that is deeper under the intact skin cannot drain onto the surface, so the pus cannot escape. This is increasingly painful and requires immediate surgical attention (see pages 115–117).

Diverticula are little pockets or balloon-like out pouchings of the colon (especially in the sigmoid). These "divs" occasionally bleed and may leave a streak of blood on the surface of the stool, but they may also bleed profusely. The blood may be a little darker red because it comes from higher up. However, an inflamed diverticulum (diverticulitis) is less likely to bleed than one that is not inflamed (see pages 59–66).

Anal intercourse may cause rectal bleeding, particularly if it is forceful, if the canal is not lubricated or if the lining is already irritated.

It is not very difficult to get an idea of the blood source from the colour and location, and therefore how serious the problem is likely to be. It is also useful to note whether there is any associated pain or swelling. But any time there is bleeding, a full examination is imperative for diagnosis. Only when the correct diagnosis has been made and the problem determined can we be sure there is no cancer and the appropriate treatment be carried out.

6

Anal Itch—Anusitis

NAL ITCH is a frequent affliction. It may occur at any age; it's not uncommon for people in their forties or fifties—or even seventies—to wonder why they never had it before. Although most people complain of itching outside the anal opening, only a few feel some irritation inside. Yet this is where it all begins. It is surprising how few people, understanding this, treat the inside.

People with anal irritation want to scratch, to rid themselves of this itch. They are often the subject of numerous cartoons and the butt of many jokes. It can be a very annoying and distracting ailment. But scratching only gets at the skin, not the source up the canal. Furthermore, it worsens the irritation and may break the skin open and cause ulcers.

Anal irritation almost always starts inside the anal canal. Because there are no pain nerves in the mucosa of the upper end of the canal, there is no pain. The external irritation is caused by a small discharge; the leakage to the outside results in stained underwear, itchiness, blood on the toilet paper and pain on sitting.

I use the term *anusitis* to describe this condition.* It refers to the irritated or inflamed mucosa of the anal canal. The mucosa is normally

---

*Anusitis is a term not yet widely used. For more information, see William W. H. Rudd, et al., "Anusitis: An Overlooked Clinical Entity" in *Canadian Family Physician*, March 1992, pages 577–578, 581.

a pale tan-pink in its upper part and skin colour in its lower part. In the presence of anusitis, both parts take on a blush-red colour. If the inflammation is severe enough, it becomes painful, although the pain can only be felt in the lower half of the canal below the dentate line. This is why so few people realize the cause originates higher up inside the canal.

Causes of Anal Itch

Although anal itching includes both *pruritis ani* and anusitis, pruritis is caused by anusitis. Of primary concern is what causes the lining of the anal canal to become inflamed (anusitis). Finding the cause and cure for anusitis will make the secondary problems of skin irritation, skin ulcers and fissuring, bleeding and discharge all disappear. Treat-

---

Frequent Causes of Anusitis

- Diet—coffee, beer, cola, garlic, pizza, spicy sauces and curry;
- Diarrhea;
- Stress.

Less Frequent Causes of Anusitis

- Excessive citrus fruits and juices—orange, grapefruit and lemon;
- Chocolate;
- Nuts;
- Popcorn;
- Red meat (except veal);
- Fatty meat (especially pork);
- Milk and milk products if the person is lactose-intolerant;
- Strawberries;
- Food preservatives;
- Food colouring.

---

ing these secondary problems is only a temporary measure. In many instances, however, only the secondary problems cause discomfort because the anusitis is located in the upper part of the anal canal, where there are no pain nerves.

By far the most frequent cause of anusitis is the *diet*. Certain foods and drinks cause irritation of the lining. In my experience, the following are the biggest offenders, in order of severity:

- *Coffee*—both regular and decaffeinated. Many people who suffer from anusitis drink as many as 15 cups of coffee a day. The cause is not caffeine—it makes no difference if the coffee is decaffeinated, and tea doesn't usually cause anusitis although it does contain caffeine.
- *Cola*—regular, decaffeinated and diet.
- *Beer*—the weekend drinker suffers more on Monday. Alcohol does not have as much effect.
- *Spicy food and garlic*—especially hot peppers, onions, Italian sauces, spaghetti sauce, pizza and curries.

Less frequent causes are *citrus drinks and fruits*, such as orange juice, grapefruit and lemon, as well as *chocolate, nuts* and *red meats*. Occasionally, food preservatives and artificial flavourings may also cause anusitis.

These irritating foods and drinks travel to the anal canal through the bloodstream and, possibly, in the stool. There may be a higher concentration in the anal mucosa because of the relatively high flow of blood. Another factor may be the susceptibility of the anal canal to damage from hard bowel movements. Other contributing factors may be changes in the bacterial, fungal or acidic environment, brought on by severe diarrhea, food poisoning, diet or a course of antibiotics.

Stress, a major cause of anusitis, seems to be on the increase in our society. Sometimes, just understanding that stress is causing the problem is enough to give considerable relief. In these cases, symptomatic treatment is all that is needed. Learning stress management, and perhaps seeking psychotherapy, will also alleviate the condition.

Antibiotics are another cause of anusitis, especially when they cause diarrhea. Usually prescribed to treat infection, they often change the normal bacterial content of the colon, thus upsetting the normal equilibrium: some bacteria are killed while others are allowed to flourish. The colon becomes sensitive to minor insults which didn't affect it before. Antibiotics should always be administered with great care because their use may lead to damage to the mucosa of the colon.

Diarrhea—multiple watery stools—usually gives anyone a sore rear end (anusitis). It only becomes a problem if the diarrhea persists longer than a day or two (see pages 45–50).

Diagnosing Anusitis

In almost every case, the irritation involves the entire circumference of the skin and mucosa of the anal canal; it is not localized to just one spot. This is what helps differentiate anusitis from other anal problems.

Two other points are worth emphasizing. First, the anal itch varies from mild (only apparent during a bowel movement) to severe (interpreted as severe pain or steady irritation). It may be so uncomfortable that it keeps people awake all night. Second, the more severe the anusitis, the more likely there are to be some secondary problems such as bleeding, fissuring or ulcers. Although many of these secondary problems can be treated, anusitis is the primary cause.

If the anusitis is *severe*, the resulting discharge flows out onto the anal skin. The moisture causes an irritation called *pruritis ani*. These two conditions are almost always seen together, although mild anusitis may be seen alone.

When the skin is sufficiently irritated, it cracks in many places, which I call *fissuring*. These small superficial splits in the skin are very painful, especially during bowel movements, but they heal quickly. This is not the same thing as an anal fissure, which has a different cause and requires different treatment (see pages 99–105).

Anal leakage is caused by the secretions from anusitis and the accompanying raw wounds of the fissuring and ulcers. There is a clear or brown discharge, with or without blood, usually seen on the toilet paper or underwear. Sometimes, people with a lot of discharge think they have lost control of their sphincter muscle—the correct diagnosis and the correct treatment can make all the difference.

Bleeding comes from the irritated lining and the damaged skin. It usually occurs during a bowel movement. This bright red blood is mostly seen on the toilet paper on wiping, but it may drip into the toilet water. Although there is usually not much blood, it is occasionally enough that it colours the toilet water red and stains the underwear. In rare cases, so much blood is lost that a blood transfusion is required. Bleeding from anusitis is often confused with piles—which may result in a misdiagnosis and even inappropriate treatment (see Chapter 4).

As with the appearance of any blood, the condition should be checked by a doctor. After taking the medical history, the doctor does a complete visual and digital examination (see pages 8–9). The most important area to examine is the anal canal. Most doctors will examine the anal canal with their gloved finger. This will reveal tenderness uniformly around the entire circumference of the anal canal, which is characteristic of anusitis. Other conditions are usually painful in one spot only.

The next step is to look at the lining of the anal canal directly with an *anoscope* and a *sigmoidoscope*. This examination should be done by someone trained to use the equipment. Correct diagnosis requires using the anoscope to look directly at the lining of both the anal canal and the lowest inch or two of the rectum. Sigmoidoscopy is done to check for lesions in the rectum and lower sigmoid colon.

Treatment of Anal Itch

Some people with anusitis are bothered more than others. They find even mild anusitis very uncomfortable; the others not at all. So treatment may not always be necessary. However, if it is bothersome, it should be treated. The first step is to concentrate on the cause of the anusitis and then deal with the secondary problems later. In the past, treatment was concentrated on the skin complaint and was therefore not very effective. The symptoms often disappeared during the treatment, only to return after it had stopped.

The longer the anal itch has been present, the harder it is to treat and the longer it takes. The most effective long-term treatment is to stop consuming the offending food or drink and to learn to manage stress. This is always more effective than treating just the secondary symptoms by using suppositories or creams; they may soothe the external skin, but they do not treat the anusitis itself.

Changing the diet means reducing consumption of the foods and drinks that are the usual offenders—coffee, beer, colas, and spices, especially when used in excess. If consuming them in small amounts doesn't help, then they must be eliminated for a period of at least 2 weeks or until the symptoms have gone. One item can be reintroduced into the diet every 3 days, to find out which is causing the anusitis. Symptoms usually take 2 or 3 days to show up. Concentrate first on coffee, colas, beer, garlic and spices. The rest are much less frequent causes. Always seek medical advice if there are any health problems that might make dieting difficult.

Diet is also a factor in keeping stools soft. For both anusitis and its secondary problems, this is very helpful. A hard stool will scrape the already tender lining and tear the damaged skin. Also, loose frequent stools, as in diarrhea, will irritate the irritated area even more. In either case, stool softeners will help restore the bowel movements to normal. The most effective stool softener is insoluble or dietary fibre—mostly from grains and some fruits and vegetables (see pages 32–33). Metamucil is often suggested, but it is evidently 90% soluble fibre and therefore not as effective.

If cutting out these items does not alleviate the condition, learning how to *manage stress better* may help. Try to avoid the stressful circumstances and learn how to handle your reaction to them. Although different methods work for different people, most benefit from relaxation techniques, regular exercise such as running, or any activity that makes them feel better about themselves. Psychotherapy or professional help in stress management may also be helpful.

A common treatment prescribed is *suppositories*, which only treat the lining of the rectum. Because the anal canal is usually collapsed (except during a bowel movement), very little medication goes down to the site of the anusitis. *Steroid creams* that soothe the skin again do not treat the anusitis but may be helpful in the treatment of pruritis ani. Steroid creams require a prescription and should only be used for a week or two at a time, to avoid damage to the skin.

Anal hygiene is important in alleviating the secondary symptoms of anusitis, such as pruritis ani. Coloured or perfumed toilet paper may irritate the skin, so *use large balls of cotton batting* to wipe and wash and pat the area dry. *Clean well after every bowel movement*; the best

---

Tips for Dealing with Anal Itchiness

- *Never scratch!* Even scratching during your sleep can perpetuate the cycle.
- *Keep the anal area dry*—by dusting with corn starch as many as six times a day. Dust before and after perspiration (e.g., after exercising).
- *Avoid oily ointments* such as Vaseline.
- *Improve your bowel habits*—aim for one to three large, soft, regular bowel movements a day by increasing your high-fibre intake and drinking plenty of water.
- *Use a glycerine suppository* just before a bowel movement if you suspect hard stool.
- *Keep at the diet and treatment* long after the symptoms have gone, to be sure the cause has been treated effectively.
- *Use Anurex* for at least two weeks after the symptoms have gone. Use Anurex before going to bed and again the following morning to prevent a recurrence if you go off your diet.

---

way is to take a shower with a mild soap such as Aveeno after every bowel movement, although that's not very convenient. Use products such as Tucks or flushable wet toilet paper to keep the area clean between showers. *Dust the area with corn starch* to keep it dry.

Regardless of the cause, something is needed to treat the irritated lining of the lower anal canal and the skin at the anal margin directly, to stop the pain and bleeding while giving the changes in diet and stress management time to work. Once the symptoms have been relieved, the causes can be determined if the condition returns after treatment is stopped. The treatment I recommend is to use a product called *Anurex* (see Figure 14). A non-prescription item available over the counter (although you may need to ask your pharmacist to order it), Anurex is a reusable anal probe (suppository stick) that contains a cold-retaining gel. It is to be cooled in the freezer of the refrigerator and then inserted into the anal canal. Because the Anurex probe makes direct contact with the entire circumference of the anal canal, it is the only method of treating the lining of the anal canal directly. A suppository treats the rectum and cream the external skin—neither treats the anal canal.

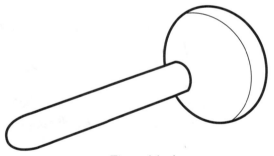

Figure 14: Anurex

Anurex was developed by Jerzy Pohler as a way of applying cryotherapy (therapeutic use of cold) to the anal canal. The cold causes the engorged blood vessels to constrict and decreases the blood flowing through them, thereby decreasing the inflammation, swelling, pain and bleeding. Although it was not intended as a treatment for anusitis, I began to use it after a patient of mine told me she had found relief by inserting a condom filled with crushed ice into her rectum. I have since conducted one study on 265 people and another blind study; both studies found Anurex to be more than 90% effective.

The Anurex probe is safe to use because the cold-retaining gel is sealed within a plastic case, which is inert. There are no chemicals, harmful antibiotics or steroids used with it to cause damage or allergic reactions. It can be used many times a day if necessary; it may lose its potency after a period of 6 months.

Because the cause of *pruritis ani* is almost always the discharge from the anusitis, the best treatment dries it up. Dusting the anal area with the ordinary *corn starch* used in cooking is the most effective way to absorb moisture. It should be reapplied many times during the day. Corn starch and Anurex are also good for treating fissuring.

Using Anurex

The Anurex probe should be stored in its container in the freezer of the refrigerator. A deep freeze is too cold. It would take an hour to cool down to the effective temperature before it could be used. A water-soluble lubricant (such as K-Y Jelly) is also required to lubricate the anal canal and the probe. The probe is then inserted into the canal and left there for 6 minutes. The first two or three times Anurex is used it might feel a little uncomfortable, as does an ice pack when applied to the face after dental work. After it is withdrawn, the probe should be washed with soap and water, put back into its container and replaced in the freezer until next time.

The best approach is to continue using Anurex for 2 weeks, even after all the symptoms have gone, to make sure the problem is solved. If the symptoms return, treat yourself with Anurex immediately, as this produces quicker results. Also, if foods likely to cause anusitis are eaten, such as beer, coffee, cola or spices, Anurex can be used afterward and again the next morning, to avoid a recurrence. In mild cases, Anurex should be used once daily for a week, either at night or after a bowel movement. In severe cases, it should be used at least twice daily for about 2 weeks and then once daily for 2 weeks after the symptoms have disappeared. If the pain is really severe, it can be used every hour if necessary, without a problem. Using two Anurex probes one after the other (for a total of 12 minutes) has occasionally been necessary to break the cycle. If the condition persists, seek medical attention.

Tips for Using Anurex

- Store in refrigerator's freezer compartment.
- Lubricate anal canal and probe with water-soluble lubricant.
- Insert for 6 minutes at a time.
- Wash thoroughly after use.
- Use after a bowel movement or at night.
- Use any time there is anal pain, even during pregnancy.

7

Anal Fissure and Anal Fistula

NAL FISSURE and anal fistula are two very different problems which are often confused. Even though anal fissures occur fairly often, most people know very little about this simple problem. Fortunately, it is easy to diagnose and treat in its early stages. Symptoms and discomfort vary from person to person and depend on the type of fissure. The word fistula sounds very similar to fissure, which may lead to confusion. Occasionally, a fissure may become a fistula, but that is as close as they get.

Anal Fissure

An anal fissure is a tear, crack or split in the skin of the lower part of the anal canal (see Figure 15). It is located just below the dentate line, in an area richly supplied by pain nerves and blood vessels. A fissure hurts and bleeds quite easily. The bright red blood is seen usually on the toilet paper or as a thin streak on the surface of the stool but sometimes in the toilet water.

It is the raw area at the base of the fissure which bleeds. Secretions and stool also collect there, resulting in a burning pain about half an hour after a bowel movement. This is different from the ripping or cutting pain sometimes felt during a large bowel movement.

A fissure is either acute or chronic. It starts off as *acute*, i.e., a fresh cut or split. There is usually only one. The skin edges are thin and soft, and the cut is usually not deep at this stage. The base of the fissure is a pink colour, and it bleeds easily. At this stage, the fissure hurts and bleeds the most. Hard stool will tend to tear the cut again—causing pain with each bowel movement. A cut in the skin elsewhere in the body can be covered by a bandage and left to heal. But the anus must be used for bowel movements, so it is more difficult to treat, keep clean and put at rest. (It is not a good idea to withhold bowel movements—this only makes it worse for next time.)

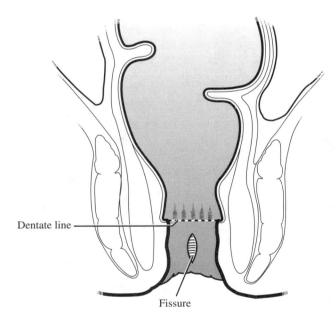

Dentate line

Fissure

Figure 15: Anal Fissure

A *chronic* fissure develops from an acute fissure that didn't heal. It takes about 3 months for a fissure to become chronic. An acute fissure can heal and/or break open again, but a chronic fissure is there for the whole 3 months or more. By that time, it has eroded down to the underlying sphincter muscle, which is now exposed. The skin edges are thickened, firm and rolled over so that the crevices underneath them are hard to see unless they are pulled apart quite hard. Also, scar tissue has grown in the side walls of the fissure. The scar tissue and underlying muscle give the chronic fissure a white appearance. Secretions and stool get trapped under the edges, resulting in more inflammation. This causes more scar tissue to form, and a vicious cycle has begun. The chronic fissure doesn't hurt or bleed as much as an acute fissure because the edges are toughened by this scar tissue, but this also prevents it from healing by itself. Sometimes a *sentinel tag* (excess bit of skin) can be seen next to the outer end of the fissure.

Fissuring, which accompanies anusitis, is the presence of multiple little cracks in the anal area; it is not the same as a fissure. These cracks are very superficial—like a paper cut—and accompanied by considerable irritation of the skin and moisture. Anusitis causes the discharge and irritation responsible for fissuring; it does not require surgery (see Chapter 6).

Causes of Anal Fissures

A fissure is almost always caused initially by a hard stool being forced out during an episode of constipation, although it may occasionally be caused by anal trauma. The anal canal is ripped or torn. A soft stool will not do this. As the body ages, the anal canal doesn't expand as easily. Indeed, children's bowel movements are often much wider than those of adults. The anal canal in some people is narrowed because of scar tissue, so it can't expand normally, or sometimes there is involuntary spasm of the sphincter muscle during a bowel movement. Also, a little bit of pain with a large bowel movement may put the sphincter into spasm and tighten it. The rest of the evacuation is then hard to push out, and the skin tears even more. Any anal canal that doesn't expand normally with a bowel movement is more likely to develop a fissure. A recurrent or continuing problem with fissures may indicate anal stenosis (see pages 37–38).

Symptoms of Anal Fissure

- Tearing pain during a bowel movement;
- Stinging pain that begins half an hour after a bowel movement;
- Streaks of bright red blood on the surface of the stool;
- Blood on toilet paper after wiping;
- Itchiness in one spot in the anal area.

Diagnosing an Anal Fissure

An acute fissure is diagnosed easily from history and symptoms alone. Typically, there is a *tearing, cutting pain*, which occurs only during a bowel movement and is caused by the stool stretching the canal as it passes. The pain subsides after the bowel movement. This pain, which feels like a knife cut, sometimes makes people try to avoid another bowel movement, but the stool only becomes larger and causes even more pain.

About one half-hour after the bowel movement, a different kind of pain occurs—a *burning or stinging pain*, due to the irritation of the secretions in the fissure. These two types of pain are quite different; the presence of both is characteristic of an acute fissure.

The pain of a fissure is *localized to one place in the anal canal*, unlike the generalized pain of anusitis. Over 90% of fissures are located in the middle at the back (in the direction of the backbone)—this is called the mid-line posterior. However, it is difficult to feel exactly where the fissure is located because no part of the anal ring is very far from any other.

Doing a digital examination can be very difficult because the fissure is so painful, especially if it is in the acute stage. In order to make the diagnosis, the skin edges of the fissure must be pulled apart; otherwise, the diagnosis may be missed and delay the treatment that will prevent the acute fissure from becoming a chronic one.

Most people, already familiar with the pain during bowel movements, immediately tighten the buttocks, the sphincter automatically going into spasm, when the doctor starts pulling. This makes it very difficult to complete the examination—in fact, sometimes the digital examination is skipped altogether.

A good trick is for you—not the doctor—to pull the buttocks apart. It works best if your finger tips are as close as possible to the anal opening so you can pull the buttocks slowly and steadily apart as far as tolerable. Because you are in control, you are less likely to cause the sphincter muscle to spasm. The doctor may need to separate the buttocks a little more on the exact spot to see the depth of the fissure. If it is painful, this is as far as the examination needs to go.

Treatment of a Fissure

The treatment depends on whether it is an acute or chronic fissure.

In its early stages, an acute fissure may have been present for only a few days or weeks. Given a chance, it should heal on its own as long as the factors that caused it are eliminated. If not, repeated damage will make it become chronic.

The most important thing is to *keep the stools small and soft*. Because laxatives can aggravate the problem and prevent healing if continued for more than a few weeks, bulk stool softeners are better. A high-fibre diet, with high-fibre cereals and lots of water, works best (see page 33).

But it might take 2 or 3 days for the high-fibre diet to start working. Even one hard bowel movement can tear the fissure again and set you back a week. *Glycerine suppositories* may be used to soften the stool in the meantime, although they might be hard to insert if the fissure is very painful.

As with anusitis, which often accompanies a fissure, it is important to *avoid certain foods* such as coffee, beer, colas and spices that irritate the anal canal. Because of the anusitis and the pain caused by the fissure itself, it is often helpful to use Anurex, the reusable cold suppository probe, to soothe the fissure by cooling (see pages 96–98). *Corn starch* applied frequently helps relieve any skin irritation and dry up any moisture.

This recommended treatment for an acute fissure should produce complete healing. After the fissure has healed, it is wise to have a further examination, to rule out any other problems that could have caused the fissure.

If an acute fissure is not treated, it will become chronic and require surgery. Very rarely, someone with an acute fissure has such severe pain that a lateral subcutaneous internal sphincterotomy should be performed under local anesthetic in the office.

The treatment of a chronic fissure is completely different. Because the skin edges of the fissure are thickened and the base has eroded down to the muscle, normal healing cannot occur. In chronic fissures, as in acute ones, the internal sphincter (the lowest part of one of the sphincter muscles) is in spasm and must be relaxed without doing damage to the external sphincter. The external sphincter is the main muscle of control.

The most effective treatment is a *lateral subcutaneous internal sphincterotomy*. This quick operation takes 3 minutes and can be done using a local anesthetic in the doctor's office. This avoids the inconvenience and expense of going to a hospital, as well as the added risk associated with a general anesthetic. No bowel preparation or clean-out is required.

One very small incision is made in the skin on one side of the opening of the anal canal (therefore usually not near the fissure). The tip of the internal sphincter is easy to find because it is in spasm. It is often thickened by some scar tissue which has formed in it. The tip of the sphincter is divided with scissors. The other muscle, the external sphincter, is not touched.

After the procedure is finished, pressure is applied to the incision with the fingers for about 5 minutes to prevent bleeding. The only dressing necessary is a bit of cotton batting. No stitches are required because the wound is made in such a way that it closes by itself, usually within 2 days. The pain is gone immediately or at least within 2 days. The procedure is so effective that many times I have heard the first post-operative bowel movement described as "a pleasure"! The fissure itself usually heals within 2 weeks, at which time any other complaints such as discharge and bleeding are also gone. Sometimes, a little more treatment, usually to remove the sentinel tag, is required. This method of sphincterotomy only requires a few minutes—very different from other procedures that involve a hospital stay, a general anesthetic, a week off work and painful bowel movements for another 3 to 4 weeks.

For example, one procedure no longer recommended involves cutting out the whole fissure, leaving a large, painful wound that requires many weeks to heal. Nor does it relax the muscle spasm directly. Another inappropriate procedure is forced anal dilatation. Although this process relaxes the sphincter spasm by stretching, it doesn't prevent a recurrence, so the fissure doesn't heal. Occasionally, the stretching damages the person's muscular control.

Anal Fistula

An anal fistula is a false passage or tunnel, under the skin of the anal margin, leading from just above the dentate line usually out to the skin near the canal (see Figure 16). The tunnel can be very superficial or so deep that it passes through some of the sphincter muscles. The superficial fistula is more common, as it results from an acute fissure in which the edges of the skin have closed over it like a bridge. The deeper fistula, which arises from an anal gland, is not seen very often but is more serious.

Causes of Anal Fistula

Anal glands are located all around the anal canal just above the dentate line and some extend through the internal sphincter muscle. Most end there, but some pass through the external muscle into a fatty space. On occasion, a gland becomes infected and develops into an *abscess*, which is an infection that extends out to the end of the gland (see pages 115–117). If the mouth of the gland in the mucosa (lining) becomes blocked off and the abscess grows, the infection travels out of the gland and out towards the skin surface, where, if left alone, it bursts through the skin to create the fistula.

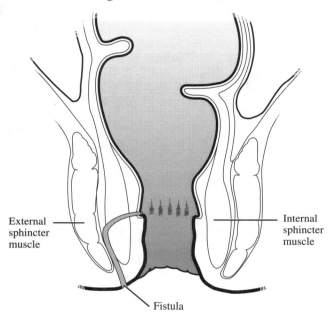

External sphincter muscle

Internal sphincter muscle

Fistula

Figure 16: Anal Fistula

Diagnosing an Anal Fistula

If an abscess is left alone, and the internal opening from the anal gland is blocked off, the abscess will enlarge in this enclosed space. This is very *painful*, and if left untreated, the abscess will burst through the skin, becoming a fistula. Then the pain is relieved. Once the abscess drains, the main symptom is *discharge* that can be white, yellow, green or brown. The first three colours usually indicate an infection; the brown means stool is coming through the internal opening and out the fistula—through an internal connection to the anal canal. This discharge is bothersome and irritating, but the severe pain is gone.

Diagnosis of an anal fistula requires a *visual examination* and is confirmed by gently passing a very fine, malleable silver *wire probe* through the tunnel from the opening in the skin towards the opening in the anal gland.

Treatment of Anal Fistula

Surgery is always necessary in order to cure a fistula. The roof of the tunnel must be removed to create a trough. This is best done by cutting (sometimes with electrocautery) down to a probe that has been inserted in the tunnel. The edges of the wound may be trimmed so they don't bulge over the wound, and the sides are cauterized to stop bleeding. In my practice, 80% of anal fistulas are treatable under local anesthetic in the office. The deeper ones require surgery in hospital. These are more dangerous because more of the muscles of anal control may be involved, and de-roofing these can harm bowel control unless special precautions are taken. In these cases, the surgery must be done in stages, and sometimes the muscle must be cut and then sewn up again.

In most cases, only a local anesthetic is required, and the postoperative period is painful only if the wound is not kept clean and dry. The wound must be cared for and watched carefully as it heals so the base fills in from the inside out before the skin edges close (see "Wound Care" on page 121). If any side channel is not opened at the time of surgery, or the skin is not pulled apart daily and bridges over, the fistula will recur.

8

Painful Anal Swellings, Skin Tags and Warts

EVEN a small amount of swelling in the tissues around the anal area can be very painful, especially if it happens suddenly. This is because these tissues are held tightly together by little fibrous bands that have no elasticity. Any swelling stretches the tissue in that area and causes pain. The larger the swelling, the bigger the stretch and hence the more pain.

There are two common kinds of swelling in this area: hematoma and abscess. Both are entirely separate entities, and both are very painful, but a hematoma is common whereas an abscess is not. A hematoma starts suddenly; an abscess starts slowly and gradually gets worse. The hematoma usually goes away by itself without treatment; an abscess needs surgery urgently. Both cause separate swellings in one part of the circle. Each has different characteristics, so by asking the proper questions it is not hard to figure out which is which.

Skin tags and warts are not painful but can be annoying at times. Skin tags are very common—most of us have small ones that don't need treatment. However, warts are caused by a virus and must be removed so they don't spread. Let's go over all of these lumps and bumps one at a time.

Hematoma

A hematoma occurs much more frequently than an abscess but is not
as serious. It is a blood clot, probably formed from a burst blood vessel. In appearance, it is a blue-black, rounded, dome-shaped swelling.
Although a person with a hematoma may feel as though the pain
comes from all around the anus, it is only in one spot. A hematoma
may be located anywhere around the circumference of the anal margin and is described as being on the left, the right, towards the back,
the front, or in any combination of these. There is usually only one
(although occasionally there are little satellite hematomas beside the
main one) or perhaps another on the other side. A hematoma occurs
mostly just at the anal margin, where the skin starts to separate, di-
verging into the buttocks, and it is always below the dentate line.
Being on the outside, it is easy to touch with the hand—especially
while wiping after a bowel movement.

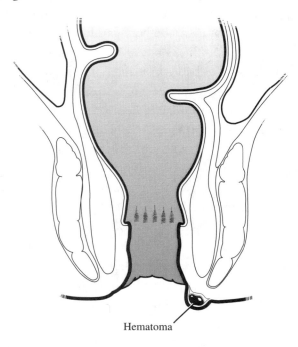

Hematoma

Figure 17: Hematoma

A hematoma is similar to a black eye. In both, the pain, discolouration and puffiness come on suddenly, caused by blood from a burst vessel that collects and then clots. The pain disappears after a few days, but the swelling and discolouration last much longer.

A hematoma is often confused with a pile (hemorrhoid), but there is a big difference between the two (see Chapter 4). A pile is located beneath the lining of the anal canal above the dentate line, where there are no pain nerves. The hematoma is located in the skin below the dentate line, where there are lots of pain nerves. A pile rarely hurts, but a hematoma almost always does (unless it is very small). Furthermore, a pile can usually be pushed back up inside completely, if it protrudes, but will come back out with the next bowel movement or, if large enough, even after standing for some time. A hematoma, by contrast, is attached to the skin on the outside and cannot be pushed back up inside completely. It goes in partially but comes right back out again.

On occasion, the hematoma can be so big (and painful) that it bursts through the skin and bleeds. The blood is usually dark red and accompanied by clots of blood, although sometimes it is bright red. The moment it bursts, the pressure is relieved and the pain is gone— for the time being. As an open wound, it will bleed for several days until the wound closes over. If it closes over too soon, the space will fill up with a clot and become painful all over again.

Causes of Hematoma

- Straining at stool;
- Heavy lifting;
- Sitting for long periods;
- Pregnancy and childbirth;
- Anusitis;
- Anal surgery;
- Diarrhea.

The larger the hematoma, the more painful it is and the longer it lasts. It sometimes grows bigger and more painful over 1 or 2 days but the pain is usually at its worst at the beginning. With proper bowel movements and an absence of irritation and straining, the pain will slowly subside over the next few days. The swelling takes a lot longer to go away—usually 2 to 3 weeks—just like a black eye.

Causes of Hematoma

A common misconception is that a pile is caused by sitting on a cold surface. This is not a pile—it is a hematoma. Anything that puts increased pressure on the blood supply or vessels in the anal area can cause a burst blood vessel in the area. Although hematomas may occur spontaneously, by far the most frequent causes of hematoma are *constipation* and *straining* at stool. The next most frequent cause is *lifting heavy objects*, such as furniture, or carrying suitcases while travelling. Not using the proper technique for *weight training* can also cause a hematoma, as can *sitting for long periods*, such as while driving a taxi or truck. Some people even consider it an occupational hazard. It also occurs very frequently late in *pregnancy or during childbirth*, when there is extra pressure bearing down in this area. After the first hematoma, less strain or pressure is required to produce another one in the same location, unless it has been removed surgically.

One possible aggravating factor is *irritation of the lining* of the anal canal—anusitis (see Chapter 6). This causes more blood to flow in dilated and weakened blood vessels, which then burst more easily. Under these circumstances, the hematoma can occur after less straining. Indeed, there may be no history of constipation or straining at all.

Another frequent cause is the *trauma* or irritation caused by having surgery in the anal area for piles, fissures or anal lesions.

Occasionally, the frequent watery bowel movements of *diarrhea* may be the irritating factor and the cause of a hematoma (see pages 45–50).

Diagnosing a Hematoma

A hematoma can usually be diagnosed accurately just from the history. In some cases, there is a warning—a localized irritated spot around the anus. More often, the swelling just happens. This may occur very suddenly or slowly over a few hours. There is usually only a single rounded swelling, which is the source of the pain.

Placing a mirror on the floor and squatting over it, a person can check for the presence of a hematoma—although it can be quite unnerving to see the blue lump.

The diagnosis is confirmed by a *visual examination*. With the person holding the buttocks apart, the doctor can easily see the swelling. No further examination at that time is needed, which is a relief because the hematoma itself is too painful. However, once the hematoma has resolved, further examinations should be made to rule out any more serious problems. A sigmoidoscopy and perhaps a colonoscopy should be done later, when the pain has subsided.

Treatment of a Hematoma

A hematoma nearly always goes away by itself. Therefore, there are two types of treatment, conservative and surgical.

The most common approach is a *conservative treatment* that uses *stool softeners* and sometimes *glycerine suppositories* to make straining during a bowel movement unnecessary. This is best done with a high-fibre diet (see page 33) or a stool softener such as Metamucil. The person should also *avoid lifting heavy objects* and *spending too much time standing or walking*, as these cause pressure and friction in the area which tends to increase the swelling.

Direct treatment of the hematoma should consist of *applying cold* to the swelling immediately, using ice or the Anurex probe. This is only effective for the first 24 to 48 hours of the hematoma. Anurex should be also used up inside the canal to soothe any anusitis that may be present. Spices, coffee, beer and cola should be avoided for a week, as they aggravate the anusitis.

Surgical treatment is only required in two circumstances: the hematoma is so large and painful that it is incapacitating and prevents the person from sleeping or leading a normal life; or the blood clot keeps coming back, always in the same location. In either case, it is important to have the appropriate surgery—which involves removing the hematoma under a local anesthetic. The doctor slowly injects the anesthetic through a fine needle and then uses an electrocautery knife to cut a round or elliptical piece of the skin over the hematoma. The hematoma is cleaned out and the piece of skin removed, and then the edges of the wound are cauterized (sealed) so that they do not bleed. This also prevents the hematoma from recurring. The wound is left wide open so that no pressure builds and must be kept clean and dry so that it is not painful (see page 121).

Many doctors still recommend simply poking a hole in the hematoma without even bothering to anesthetize the area. This is not only unnecessarily painful, it is also ineffective. Under the skin of the hematoma, there may be several small clots giving the appearance of one large clot; these clots are difficult to remove through a small hole. Also, the hole closes too quickly, and the cavity fills up with blood again, becoming painful by the next day.

Sometimes the hematoma is so large and the pressure so great that it bursts on its own. Should it be left alone or removed? No hard and fast rule exists for this situation, which is not urgent, because the pain is relieved and there is little risk of infection. The hematoma should be removed if it has occurred in the same place before, if the hole in the skin is small, if the hematoma continues to bleed or if the hole is likely to close quickly and just fill up again with blood. It is important to have the hematoma examined to be sure it isn't something else.

Abscess

The other painful swelling that occurs in the anal area is an abscess, but it occurs much less frequently than a hematoma. An abscess requires prompt medical attention. Untreated, it can seriously damage the sphincter muscle unless it bursts through the skin and becomes a fistula (see pages 105–107).

An abscess is a boil or infection that creates pus in one area. Although it feels as though it is in the middle of the anal opening, it actually starts in the wall of the canal. The *pain* and *swelling* of an abscess start slowly and gradually increase, unlike a hematoma, which usually starts to become less painful after 2 or 3 days. Usually, associated *fever, lack of energy* and *tiredness* are present because of the infection.

An abscess may develop either near the anal canal next to the surface of the skin or farther away from the anal canal and deeper inside. Fortunately, a deep abscess occurs less frequently, although it is more serious. The deeper it is, the longer it takes to come to the surface and form a lump and the more damage it can do on the way.

Cause of an Abscess

An anal abscess starts in an *infected anal gland*. These glands are located above the dentate line anywhere around the circumference of the anal canal into which they open. They are like little balloons, with one opening at the anal canal and the other blind end extending outwards through the sphincter muscles. When the gland becomes infected, its opening in the canal often becomes blocked so that the infection can only extend outwards. If the infected gland is short and only goes through one layer of sphincter muscle, the abscess extends to the skin right near the anal margin and is called *superficial*. This is easy to treat because it doesn't involve cutting much muscle.

However, if the infected gland passes through both sphincter muscles, it will track out to the skin much farther away from the anal opening. This is a *deep abscess*, which is more painful than a superficial abscess. Surgery is needed urgently to relieve the terrible pain and prevent damage to the sphincter muscles.

It is important to realize that the gland's opening in the anal canal may still be open, and there may still be a tunnel (fistula) that continues to feed the infection from the bowel. This will not close or stay closed without surgery. A fistula occurs in just over half the abscesses (see pages 105–107).

Diagnosing an Anal Abscess

After taking a history, the doctor does a *visual and digital examination* to confirm the diagnosis. With the person holding the buttocks apart, the doctor can see and feel the abscess better. It is also helpful if the person identifies where in the anal circle it hurts most. If the abscess is deep, the doctor will gently feel different parts of the circumference of the anal skin, often with one finger inside the anal canal to determine which area is the most tender and to locate the swelling.

A very deep abscess can sometimes be felt only between the thumb outside and the index finger inside the canal. The doctor will probably check for a fever and may do a blood test to confirm the infection.

Treatment of an Anal Abscess

Surgery is necessary for all abscesses. The abscess must be drained. I do not recommend a course of antibiotics first, especially as the abscess, already developed, is so painful. If the abscess is untreated, part of the sphincter muscle may be eroded by the pressure, causing permanent loss of muscle control of the anal sphincter.

Most abscesses can be treated using a local anesthetic in the doctor's office, thereby avoiding the expense and inconvenience of a hospital stay, as well as the risks associated with general anesthetic. It also means prompt relief of pain and discomfort and prevents the abscess from spreading deeper into the tissues. The procedure should never be done without a local anesthetic.

As with a hematoma, the abscess should be de-roofed. Local anesthetic is injected through a fine needle into the thin skin of the abscess. A round or elliptical piece of skin is removed using electrocautery, and then the edges of the wound are treated to stop bleeding and to prevent the skin from bridging over and forming a fistula.

Once the roof is removed, the wound is left wide open so that the pus can drain; it is important for the discharge of pus to continue after the operation. The incision must not close over too quickly—after all, the whole idea is to release the pus. The discharge and a little bit of bleeding will continue until the wound has healed over. This will take a few weeks.

To prevent the need for further surgery, the edges of the wound should be separated regularly so that it heals properly. This simply means pulling the edges of the wound apart with the fingers 2 to 3 times a day.

The doctor should follow up closely after the surgery, to make sure that the wound heals from the inside out; examining the wound with a very fine silver wire probe will determine whether the passage between the anal canal and the bowel is closing completely. If the skin bridges over before the wound fills in, the abscess may recur. If the connection between the anal gland and the bowel remains open, the infection will continue to be fed from the contents of the bowel. This occurs in about 60% of cases. If the channel does not fill in from the inside out, a fistula will form, requiring further surgery.

Skin Tags

Are you familiar with the expression "smooth as a baby's bottom"? We start out in life with a nice smooth bottom, but as we get older, most of us end up with irregular bits of skin hanging around.

Skin Tags versus Hematomas

	Skin Tag	*Hematoma*
Occurrence	Frequent	Infrequent
Duration	Permanent	Intermittent
Duration of swelling	1 to 3 hours	Weeks
Contents	Empty or fluid	Blood clot
Painfulness	Mild, only when swollen	Yes
Surgery	Rarely required	Sometimes required

A skin tag is an excess piece, or tag, of skin located in any part of the circumference of the anal margin where the skin begins to separate away into the buttocks (see Figure 18).

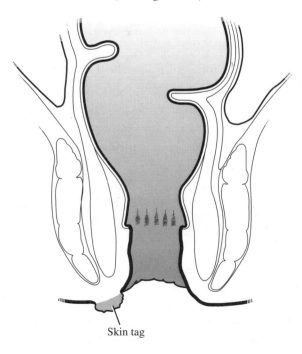

Skin tag

Figure 18: Skin Tag

The skin tag, usually collapsed (loose) and wrinkled, may fill up at times with blood (hematoma) or edema fluid. Edema fluid is fluid from tissues without any red blood cells. A large skin tag may have enough moisture between it and the adjacent skin to cause it to break open from friction. Any open ulcer in skin secretes a watery fluid, which may cause irritation in the area.

Cause of Skin Tags

The skin around the anal margin is smooth and regular when we are young. The older we get and the more bowel movements we have, the more the anal canal stretches and contracts. After many stretches, some of the elasticity in the skin is lost: it doesn't tighten up as it used to. This leaves behind small bits of excess skin, which may be filled with edema fluid or blood. Edema fluid is absorbed faster than blood—usually within 2 to 3 hours. After the swelling comes and goes a few times in the same place, the bit of stretched skin ends up as a skin tag.

Each time the same skin tag becomes swollen, the skin is stretched and becomes larger after the edema fluid has subsided. This is how skin tags get bigger and bigger over time. Sometimes, a swollen tag may be uncomfortable or even painful. A few tags get so big they make it hard to wipe clean after a bowel movement. Gone is the smooth appearance of a baby's bottom.

The factors causing this swelling are the same ones that cause a hematoma: straining at stool from *constipation* (see pages 27–36), *lifting heavy objects* such as furniture or baggage, *weight training* and *standing for long periods*. *Anusitis*, in which the lining of the anal canal is irritated, also aggravates the area (see Chapter 6).

Another important and frequent contributing factor is *sitting on the toilet* too long. This puts all the pull of gravity on the anal area, and over time edema fluid and swelling may result in either one or two swellings. It also sometimes causes the whole circumference to become swollen—perianal edema, a rare condition discussed later.

Diagnosing a Skin Tag

"Skin tag" is a good descriptive term. You can see and feel an excess bit of skin which is usually collapsed. In this state, it looks like an excess "dog ear" of skin. It has the same colour and texture as the surrounding skin. When it is full of edema fluid, however, it becomes large and full, appearing swollen and rounded and firm but not hard to the touch. It is not very painful. Once a skin tag begins to swell, the swelling will occur after a bowel movement easily and more frequently than a hematoma, and it will go away more quickly, too.

A collapsed skin tag is easy to see during a *visual examination*, but because the swelling goes away so quickly, it can be difficult for the doctor to confirm the diagnosis. Yet, it is important to make sure the swelling is not a hematoma. Ideally, the person will have a bowel movement at the doctor's office so that the doctor can see the swelling. Some doctors will even join the person in the washroom—this may be awkward, but it is the best way to understand the problem so that it can be treated properly.

Treatment for Skin Tags

Most adults have skin tags but aren't bothered by them. It really doesn't matter if the skin is not as smooth as a baby's bottom—a few small skin tags are of no consequence and do not require treatment. The conservative treatment is to *leave them alone* and keep them clean and dry.

Surgery is only necessary under two circumstances: first, if a skin tag becomes so large that it prevents proper cleaning and hygiene or creates moisture that irritates the skin in the area; second, if the skin tag becomes repeatedly swollen after bowel movements or on standing and interferes with normal activities. The surgery can be done in the doctor's office and is the same whether the skin tag is swollen or not. Local anesthetic is slowly injected into the area through a fine needle. The excess skin is then cut away, usually by *electrocautery*, which uses a hot knife or a wire loop through which electric current passes. This cuts off the tag and stops the bleeding. Electrocautery is much easier, cheaper and quicker than laser treatment, also sometimes suggested. Most activities can usually be resumed within a day of surgery, although it's wise to rest for a day or so because the friction of walking may irritate the wound.

Post-operative care is very important (see "Wound Care"). The wound must be kept clean and dry; otherwise, it becomes irritated and sore because secretions or stool do not get cleaned out.

Wound Care

The best way to clean the wound is in the shower. Imagine the area as being like the folds of an accordion, with the wound right in the bottom of a pleat. The accordion must be pulled apart to expose the wound. If you bend over in the shower with your buttocks facing the shower head, the water can pour directly onto the wound. Place the fingertips of both hands right at the edges of the wound and pull as far apart as you can, until it hurts. The wound can then be gently and thoroughly washed using soap and water (several times if necessary). Although sitz baths, which require immersing the buttocks in water, are sometimes recommended, they are not very effective because the buttocks stay pressed together—so the wound remains closed. If you can't clean the wound yourself, ask a family member or nurse to apply hydrogen peroxide right into the wound with a cotton swab (like a Q-tip) while you hold the edges of the wound apart.

Cleaning the wound should begin the day after the operation. After being washed and dried gently with a clean towel, the wound must then be kept dry by being dusted with ordinary corn starch. Do not use perfumed powders, as they could irritate the wound. The easiest way to do this is to sit on the edge of the toilet seat and push over to one side. With one hand, pull the opposite buttock away to pull the wound as far apart as possible (it might be easier to reach between the legs). With the other hand, dust the corn starch right into the wound. The corn starch should be applied at least twice a day and after a bowel movement. Some wounds are moist and leak fluid in the first week or two. This is good. Moist ones should have corn starch applied as often as necessary—as often as six times a day. If the powder gets caked, it can be washed off in the shower.

The wound must also be allowed to fill in from inside out before the skin grows across, especially if it is deep. To make sure this happens, pull the edges of the wound apart at least once daily so that they do not bridge over before the wound has filled in. Do not stop pulling the moment it starts to hurt. A little bit of pain now will prevent a lot more pain later. The opposite also holds true—if the pulling apart doesn't hurt at all, the wound is not being spread far enough.

It takes a few weeks for the wound to heal. The bigger and the deeper the wound, the longer it takes. But the cleaner and dryer it is, the faster it will heal.

Recurrent Perianal Edema

Perianal edema is so rare it is hardly worth mentioning. Indeed, it is often missed by the doctor, even though diagnosis may be easy, especially if swelling is present during an examination. Perianal edema is sometimes confused with piles (hemorrhoids). A proper diagnosis is necessary to make sure the symptoms are not caused by a prolapsed rectum (see pages 41–42).

The term "perianal" means that the swelling is around the entire circumference of the anal margin, below the dentate line. Perianal edema differs from a swollen skin tag in covering the entire anal circumference, whereas the skin tag is only in one or two spots.

Usually, some swelling is noticed after straining at stool or after standing all day. The swelling is not painful, but it is uncomfortable and aggravating and hard to wipe clean. It might also feel full, as though there is some stool inside the anal canal or as though there is stool left after a bowel movement (non-completion), although straining produces nothing. The swelling and feeling of fullness go away after a while. Some people sit on the bed or lie down after a bowel movement for half an hour until they feel more comfortable, which of course can be very inconvenient.

It is not clear what causes perianal swelling. There may be an inherited weakness in the area, but the more consistent factors are probably straining hard at stool, standing for long periods and sitting longer than necessary on the toilet. A good time to see the doctor for this problem is at the end of the day. It's even better if you have a bowel movement at the doctor's office so that the doctor can see the swelling and make an accurate diagnosis and hence prescribe appropriate treatment.

Treatment of Perianal Edema

Perianal edema requires hospital *surgery* to remove the loose tissue and excess skin. The surgery is like a face-lift, only at the other end. An incision is made on each side of the swelling and the flaps lifted up and cleaned out. Then the skin is sewn back together and re-attached to the underlying tissues. Unlike the surgery for abscesses or hematomas, this wound does not need to be separated and cleaned out, although the area should be kept clean and dry.

The recovery period can be painful, especially if there is a bowel movement with hard stool. The person stays in hospital for a few days and also uses stool softeners such as mineral oil and increased fibre in the diet for 2 to 3 weeks, to avoid putting any stress on the wound.

Anal Warts

Anal warts—or *condylomata acuminata*—are similar to the wart commonly seen on the hand. There might be just one or there might be many covering the whole anal area. They start out in one spot but, if left untreated, spread out like a carpet, often growing in the moist crevices of skin folds. Their colour varies from tan to white and they are not painful, although they may be itchy and, if rubbed, may bleed a little.

Anal warts are caused by a virus. They can be found in other moist areas such as the outer part of the vagina, on the penis, in the corners of the mouth and in the underarms. It is not very contagious and, like all viruses, dies on contact with air. Warts take 1 to 11 months to grow after contact, so the virus may be present long before a wart develops—the first indication that anything is wrong.

Anal warts are a sexually transmitted disease. The virus is most likely spread by repeated sexual contact. Anal warts are common in gays, particularly those who engage in anal intercourse with multiple partners. The rate at which they grow and multiply varies from person to person, probably depending on the individual's resistance; just as with the common cold, some people are more immune than others to the virus. In those with low resistance, the warts may grow quickly and double within months. In others, it may take at least 6 months or more.

The cauliflower-like raised appearance of the wart makes diagnosis easy by visual examination. They feel firm, slightly raised and have a slightly irregular texture. They don't swell after a bowel movement, as a skin tag does, but feel the same day after day as they slowly grow. You might be able to tell for yourself if you use a mirror to check the area (of course, you might need to be a bit of a contortionist!). Most people don't know the warts are there until they notice them after wiping themselves—by then the virus has usually been present for some time. In the later stages, it may become difficult to wipe the area clean after a bowel movement. As a result, the moist secretions and stool that collect there irritate the skin, perhaps resulting in ulcerations and blood. This rawness is the only pain associated with anal warts.

Although diagnosis is usually easily confirmed just by inspecting the area, the anal canal should be examined using an anoscope to see if there are any warts inside the anal canal. Usually, they extend about an inch (3 cm) into the anal canal. The rest of the genitals, as well as the underarms and the sides outside the mouth, should also be inspected to make sure there are no other warts; if found, they must also be treated. It is important that the infected person's sexual partner also be checked for warts. If necessary, a wart can be removed under local anesthetic and the diagnosis confirmed under the microscope. The diagnosis is harder in the early stages, when only one or two warts are present, than in the later stages, when large numbers are.

Treatment of Anal Warts

Anal warts do not go away on their own, but there are several methods of treating them. The simplest—but slow—method is to *apply an acid* to the wart with a small stick. This method is used most often, especially on very small warts, and can be done in the doctor's office. An acid compound of *podophyllin* or *bichloracetic acid* (BCA) is rubbed on the wart with an applicator. The chemicals burn the tissue but don't penetrate very deeply, although BCA penetrates further than podophyllin. Podophyllin must be washed off a few hours later because it will continue to burn any normal skin it comes in contact with. Either compound must be carefully applied to the wart and the normal skin avoided. It is only a little painful if the chemical contacts some of the raw area left from a previous application. This treatment must be repeated every 2 weeks until the warts are gone. After a week, the warts fall off, leaving raw spots that heal within a few weeks as the skin grows out from the bridges of normal skin between the warts. As with any method of treatment, an anoscope should be used to look for any warts inside the canal so that they can be treated; otherwise, the outside ones will recur.

Cryotherapy (therapeutic application of extreme cold), using a liquid nitrogen spray, is faster but more costly, so it is not used very often. It requires equipment usually found in the office of a dermatologist, who is unlikely to have an anoscope and therefore usually doesn't treat any warts inside the anal canal. The nitrogen is applied precisely to the wart to avoid damage to the surrounding skin. Cryotherapy does not usually require anesthetic, although the application can be a bit painful, especially in the presence of raw areas from the previous treatments.

Electrocautery is the most effective method of treating warts, especially at the beginning of treatment if the warts are large or there is a massive number of them. It is also effective at the end of treatment if the warts are all in one area. It must be done using an injected local anesthetic, unlike the other methods, but it can be done at the doctor's office. Although the injection of anesthetic hurts, burning off the warts doesn't, and they can all be removed—even the large ones. The large warts are snipped off with scissors at the base; the smaller ones are burned off. This requires accuracy and good visibility: it is very important to hold the buttocks apart so that the doctor can burn only the warts and not the bridges of healthy skin. Each wart removed leaves behind a small wound that will be painful if not kept clean and dry.

It is important to *refrain from sexual contact* during the treatment for anal warts so that the virus does not spread. Refraining also helps to prevent reinfection.

It is also important to *keep the area clean and dry*, since the virus loves moisture. It is best cleaned in a shower (not a bath) twice a day with soap and water and patted dry. Applying corn starch between 2 and 6 times a day, as frequently as necessary, keeps the area dry.

I sometimes recommend taking 250 mg of *vitamin C and zinc tablets* once daily with food for 2 to 3 weeks. This may help fight the virus just as it helps some people fight the common cold (a different virus).

Regardless of whether chemical therapy, cryotherapy or electrocautery is used, treatment only gets rid of the warts and not necessarily all the virus. Although each time a wart is removed, the virus is killed at that spot, the virus often exists somewhere else and just has not yet developed into a wart—it can't be seen until it has grown. That is why treatments must be repeated every 2 weeks until after the warts are all gone; the area should be examined 1 month later and again 3 months later to make sure the warts haven't come back. After 3 months, if there are any more warts they are almost certainly from new, repeated sexual contact with an infected partner.

No matter which method is used, post-operative care is very important. Each wart leaves behind a raw spot; if there were many warts, that means many wounds. If the wounds are well looked after and kept clean and dry, there will be little pain and the wounds will heal more quickly (see "Wound Care" on page 121).

A fourth method of treating anal warts—*laser treatment*—I do not recommend. Similar to electrocautery, it is vastly more expensive and much slower. It also usually needs to be done in hospital. In my opinion, it's like hiring an elephant to kill a flea. This is one instance when using a laser is no improvement over the older methods.

Researchers are working on a *vaccine* that produces antibodies against that person's virus. This is also very expensive and can be done only in a few highly specialized centres and for some people. It is not effective enough to be worthwhile at this time.

Other Swellings

A *sentinel tag* is an excess bit of skin near the outer end of a fissure (see pages 105–107). Occasionally, cancer develops in the anal area. This might be mistaken for a skin tag, but it is hard and irregular to the touch; unlike a skin tag, it doesn't come and go.

As with any other condition, it is wise to have any swelling or bleeding in the anal area checked by a doctor. Early diagnosis means early treatment, preventing serious complications later.

9

Colon Cancer— Polyps and Prevention

T HE CONCEPT that most colon cancer is now preventable is the most exciting development in colon cancer treatment in this century. That this is so is one of my main reasons for writing this book—more people should know. It is worth the extra effort to prevent colon cancer for several reasons.

Colon cancer is an all too common disease. It affects 5 to 6% of both men and women—that's 150,000 a year—in North America alone. One in 20 of us. Almost half die of the disease. Over the past 50 years, very little progress has been made to improve the survival rate, despite all the "advances" in surgery, chemotherapy and radiotherapy.

Also, colon cancer is the only internal cancer that has a precursor—a polyp or growth that is not malignant but may turn into a cancer. If we can find these benign polyps and remove them before they turn bad, we are preventing colon cancer. Very few will slip by a proper follow-up routine. No other cancer of an internal organ (such as lung, breast, ovary or prostate) has a pre-malignant lesion whose removal would prevent cancer—in these other organs the cancer is already present when any abnormal growth is discovered.

Another good reason to prevent colon cancer is that few people will need to have an operation—let alone go to hospital—or go through the pain and worry of losing time from work and family.

Removing the polyp before cancer develops is far better than finding the cancer early. Still, removing a cancerous growth early gives a better prognosis, especially if there were no symptoms. After a cancerous tumour is removed from the colon, the 5-year survival rate is only about 20% if there were symptoms of pain or bleeding when the cancer was found. That's a big difference from the 80% survival rate if there were no symptoms when the cancer was found.

We've entered a new era of cancer prevention. Statistically, colon cancer is probably the second most deadly cancer in men and women who don't smoke and the third most deadly in those who do, but it is the only one that can be prevented in most cases.

Most Frequent Types of Fatal Cancer

Although there are other types of cancer that occur more frequently, colon cancer is among the top three causing death. In the overall population (including smokers) cancer deaths are as follows:

Men	*Women*
Lung	Lung
Prostate	Breast
Colon	Colon

How Cancer Grows

In order to prevent colon cancer, it is important to understand how cancer grows and what a polyp is. In fact, this polyp-to-cancer sequence forms the basis for my recommendations.

All colon cancers start in a polyp, according to one of the world's most prominent colon pathologists, Dr. Basil Morson of England. Hence our emphasis on finding polyps. We now know that the whole process of developing a polyp and having it grow into a cancer that spreads requires changes in the genes within a cell. In each cell, there are genes attached to the chromosomes that direct the activity of that cell; for cancer to develop, several genes must be either absent or mutate (change). When these genes are not present or are abnormal, cells can proliferate out of control—nothing will keep them in check.

For colon cancer to occur, there must be between six and ten different abnormal genes in a cell. The first one is called a *trigger gene* and either is abnormal at birth (as it is in one of 5,000 births) or mutates to become abnormal and start the whole process. A second gene normally keeps cell growth at a rate which is just enough to replenish the old cells. This gene also changes, allowing the cells to duplicate out of control. A third gene normally keeps the cells growing at the appropriate rate to contain them within that area, but when this gene becomes ineffective, the cancer cells also grow and spread uncontrollably. Then a fourth gene, which usually keeps the cells from spreading out though the bloodstream or going to another organ (*metastasizing*), must also be defective. Genetic scientists suspect there are a few more genes yet to be identified that must be abnormal in order for a polyp to form and turn into spreading cancer.

What causes all these changes is not known. Possible factors are congenital conditions, diet (including intake of fibre, fat and sugar) and bowel habits (particularly constipation and the amount of time stool has contact with the lining of the colon).

Obviously, if the cancer cells spread enough to take over the normal cells of another organ, such as the liver, this organ will fail to perform its vital activity. In the case of the liver, this involves detoxifying waste and poisons from the bowel and creating proteins, steroids and chemicals including bile—all of which are necessary for life. When the liver is taken over by cancer, the person becomes jaundiced, loses weight and, ultimately, dies.

Another way colon cancer kills is by growing large enough to block the bowel and cause obstruction. This can be relieved by surgery but only temporarily, because the cancer has usually spread beyond the tumour that is removed.

What is a Polyp?

A polyp in the colon is a proliferation of abnormal cells that have grown from, and are attached to, the lining of the colon and protrude into the lumen of the colon. The growth can be shaped like a wart, a cauliflower or even a mushroom (see Figure 19). A polyp is usually *benign* (not cancerous) but it can become *malignant* (cancerous). Some polyps are flat and sit right on the wall like a mat attached over a wide area (*sessile*). Some are attached by a long, thin stem like a cherry on a stalk (*pedunculated*). Still other polyps look like something in between (*marble-like*).

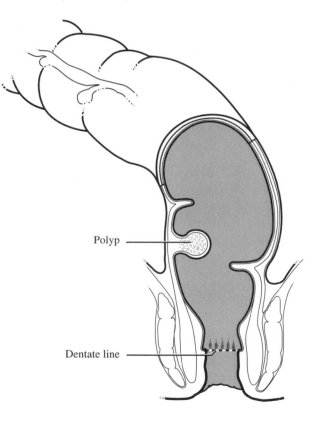

Polyp

Dentate line

Figure 19: Polyp

All colon cancers come from polyps, although not all polyps turn into cancer. But as cancer develops and grows in a polyp, it replaces the benign tissue, and this polyp may no longer be recognizable.

Some polyps turn into a cancer earlier than others. Their type and shape determine how quickly cancer can spread to adjacent normal tissue. In a pedunculated polyp with a long stalk, the cancer has much farther to go before it even reaches the wall of the bowel. This is usually less serious than cancer in a flat polyp. Also, some polyps grow slowly and some grow quickly, but the larger the polyp the more likely it is to contain cancer.

How common are polyps? Almost one-third of people over age 50 have at least one polyp. Forty percent of us will have at least one polyp during our lifetime and approximately *one-quarter of those polyps become cancer within 20 years.*

Polyps usually have no symptoms, but they can get big enough to partly block the colon and cause cramps. Some polyps bleed a little, leaving a streak of blood on the surface of the stool. Some bleed into the bowel, but this is unusual.

There are two categories of polyp: hyperplastic and adenomatous. A *hyperplastic polyp* is a small heap of cells which will disappear on their own. Although this kind of polyp is of no consequence, usually it must be removed to make sure it is not a more significant kind. *Adenomatous* polyps are three different types: tubular, villous and tubulovillous.

Tubular polyps have either a marble or a mushroom shape. They grow slowly, and probably fewer than a quarter of them turn into cancer. They can take up to 20 years to become cancerous, although rarely a polyp will become cancerous in as little as a year. These polyps are usually easy to remove by colonoscopy.

The *villous* polyp coats the lining of the bowel like a throw carpet which is stuck to broadloom. The polyp is in close contact with the lining and covers a wide area, so it can be difficult to remove. A villous polyp can turn into cancer quickly—even before it is an inch in diameter, when 50% have cancer in them. In fact, 30 to 70% of villous polyps have cancer in them when they are first found.

Tubulovillous polyps have the components and features of both. Their prognosis is between the two.

Familial polyposis is a rare, inherited disease in which hundreds of polyps cover the colon and rectum. In nearly all cases, cancer is present before the person reaches age 40. The polyp-to-cancer sequence develops spontaneously in most people without a family history; others probably have a little help from an inherited gene, necessary for this chain of events. This is why family history, including the age at which family members died from colon cancer, is so important—the earlier the condition occurs, the greater the risk.

Symptoms of Colon Cancer

At an early stage of colon cancer, there is usually no *bleeding*, although this will often occur at a later stage. Bleeding that occurs early is often overlooked as an indication of cancer, since it is thought to be caused by anusitis, piles, colitis or something else. Blood from a cancerous polyp can be bright or dark red. Dark red blood comes from high up in the colon and turns dark because it has been in the colon long enough to lose its oxygen and be changed by chemical reactions in the bowel. If the tumour is low in the bowel and the stool comes out quickly, the blood is bright red. Blood that covers part of the stool or is mixed up in it, especially if it is dark red, could be from cancer.

Persistent *cramps or swelling* in the same location in the abdomen give another warning of a possible growth in the colon. In this situation, the growth may be large enough to partially block the bowel, causing the cramps, which increase in severity and frequency as the tumour grows.

If the cancer is low in the bowel, it may create a sensation of *bearing down* in the rectum like the urge to have a bowel movement. The growth may be big enough to feel like a piece of stool that has to come out. The bowel cannot tell the difference between a growth and some stool.

Other problems such as an *inflamed lining* of the rectum also give the symptoms of fullness or bearing down and the feeling of not being finished after a bowel movement (*non-completion*).

A more subtle symptom is a *change in bowel habits*. Although bowel habits may change for many other reasons, this is quite characteristic of colon cancer. The word to emphasize here is *change*. For instance, someone with a long history of constipation may suddenly develop diarrhea or a person with regular bowel movements at the same time every day may suddenly become irregular.

In someone with a good appetite, *weight loss* suggests that cancer is consuming a lot of energy for its own growth. Furthermore, a decreased appetite may indicate that the tumour has spread to other organs, especially the liver. The vital functions of those organs become impaired.

But all these symptoms of colon cancer are only present when the cancerous tumour is quite large and has been growing for months or even years.

Of course, many other conditions cause cramps and rectal bleeding. The most common are inflammatory conditions or infections. These other causes must be ruled out by doing stool cultures; looking for parasites; and doing a colonoscopy to examine the lining of the colon, take a biopsy (sample) or remove polyps for examination under a microscope.

When people have the symptoms of obstruction (abdominal pain and swelling), changed bowel habits, weight loss or obvious bleeding, their tumour has probably been growing for a long time. By then, it is large and may have spread. In such advanced cancer, the survival rate 5 years after surgery is less than 20%.

On the other hand, if a cancerous polyp is found in someone without any of these symptoms during a routine investigation, it is more likely to be in a very early stage. In these cases, the 5-year survival rate after surgery is more than 80%—a difference of 60%. Survival is even greater if the polyp removed has not yet developed cancer—it is 100%. Which group would you rather be in?

5-Year Survival Rates for Colon Cancer

These rates apply to polyps and growths found and removed during a colonoscopy.

Polyp with no symptoms of cancer	100%
Polyp containing cancer that has not yet spread beyond the polyp	95%
Cancerous tumour found that has not spread	60%
Advanced colon cancer	20%

Treatment for Colon Cancer

Once a person has colon cancer, surgery is by far the best treatment—cut it out and get rid of it before it spreads. Colon cancer in its early stage, before it has spread, is treated by a simple operation done in hospital under anesthesia. An incision is made in the abdomen and the cancerous part of the bowel is cut away; the divided sections of bowel are then joined back up.

It is not quite so simple if the cancer is low in the rectum. There may not be enough healthy bowel left at the lower end to attach to the cut edge of the colon above. In this situation, the person ends up with a permanent *colostomy*—the end of the bowel is brought out through the skin. Stool is then evacuated through the opening and collected in a special bag, or an *enema* is self-administered every day or two to empty the colon. People who can give themselves their own high enemas usually do not need to wear a colostomy bag.

Surgery is usually the best way to treat a moderately advanced cancer, but it may be followed by radiation and chemotherapy, which are beyond the scope of this book. If you need to decide whether to have these extra treatments done, I recommend you make sure the procedure will help relieve pain or improve survival first, because radiation and chemotherapy can cause a great deal of pain and discomfort.

Prevention of Colon Cancer

For 50 years, doctors have been correctly taught that the only way to decrease the number of deaths from colon cancer is to find it at an early stage. This is because the cancer will not yet have spread, and surgery will cure the person. Even though there may be a long delay between the beginning of a cancerous growth and the time it is big enough to cause symptoms, nothing will help find and diagnose it in this quiet stage as well as colonoscopy. This means looking with an instrument directly at the inner lining of the colon and rectum by colonoscopy and sometimes at the rectum by sigmoidoscopy. Then it is possible to find a polyp and remove it right away, long before cancer can develop or symptoms can appear. That means it is possible to prevent most colon cancer just by having routine examinations.

General screening programs for colon cancer are not very dependable for early detection because they may miss some cancerous growths or polyps that do not bleed at the time the test is done. By far, the best way to prevent colon cancer is by direct vision made possible by colonoscopy.

The only drawback is having to convince people who feel perfectly well that they should undergo a colonoscopy and sigmoidoscopy regularly. I have not found this easy. They don't believe anything could be wrong if they have no complaints. Some will even avoid a routine examination for fear there might be something wrong. But my response to them is always: a little precaution now may save a lot of pain and suffering later.

That is why I feel so strongly about this issue, and why this is the most important section in this book. Any polyp can turn into cancer, and all colon cancer comes from polyps: so all we need to do is find those polyps and remove them before the cancer starts. *Colonoscopy* is the best and most accurate method for finding growths in the colon; it has the added advantage of allowing us to remove the polyp on the spot. Three times more lesions are found by colonoscopy than by x-ray. A *barium enema x-ray* produces a black-and-white picture that may not reveal all the growths; if there is anything suspicious in the x-ray, a colonoscopy is required anyway, to examine the area and take a biopsy or remove it. In fact, for these reasons x-rays are no longer preferred. These examinations are all explained in Chapter 1.

During the examination, if a lesion is found, the doctor will take a sample (*biopsy*) and remove the growth, and place them in a formalin solution to preserve them. These then go to a pathologist, who examines them under a microscope to determine whether the growth is benign or malignant. When the doctor removes a polyp, a pathologist should also examine it under the microscope.

When to Get Which Test

This is the timetable I recommend for people who have no symptoms, who have had no polyps or colon cancer in the past, and who have no family history of polyps or colon cancer.

	Age	*Repeat*
Rigid Sigmoidoscopy	age 30 to 45	Every 2 years
	age 45 and up	In between colonoscopies
Colonoscopy	age 45 and up	2 years after the first one at age 45 and then every 1 to 5 years, depending on whether polyps are found

In people with no history of polyps or colon cancer, I recommend beginning routine rigid sigmoidoscopies every 2 years from age 30. Colonoscopy should first be done at age 45 and repeated 2 years later and from then on every 3 to 5 years, with a sigmoidoscopy once in between. If a polyp or cancerous growth is found, or if the colon was not adequately cleaned out for the examination, a repeat examination is recommended within 1 year.

In people with a family history of polyps or colon cancer, the whole routine should start at least 5 years earlier.

Colonoscopies should be carried out in everyone, both male and female, who is healthy and mobile, beginning at age 45 even up to the 80s. Removing a polyp during a colonoscopy, even in an elderly person, is easier and less risky than the abdominal surgery with a bowel resection that would be required if a cancerous polyp were allowed to grow. However, tumours grow more slowly in the elderly.

Diet and Colon Cancer

Another factor in preventing colon cancer is diet. Drs. D. Burkitt and N. Painter, the researchers who studied the differences between the diets of people in rural Uganda and people in Britain, found a striking difference in the incidence of colon cancer. (For the purposes of this book, I think it's safe to assume that the North American diet is similar to the British.) The researchers noticed that the fibre intake of the Ugandans was far greater than that of the British. They also measured the weight of the stool—no mean feat, surely— and found that the Ugandans produced far more frequent and much bulkier stools. I remember a lecture given by Dr. Burkitt in Toronto at which he proclaimed that almost any rural African could produce a half-pound stool on request.

It has been reported that 50% of the British take laxatives at some time. Another study done in Britain on elderly patients in a nursing home showed that up to 3 weeks might elapse before something taken by mouth came out the other end. Now it appears there is a connection between how long stool stays in the colon and the incidence of colon cancer. Stool passes faster through the upper part of the colon, where it is more watery, and more slowly through the lower end, where it is stored in a solid form until evacuation.

Painter and Burkitt postulated that the longer it takes for stool to pass through the colon and out the rectum, the more likely it is for colon cancer to develop if any cancer-producing chemicals are present in the stool. Furthermore, colon cancer occurs a little more often at the lower end of the colon and in the rectum, where solid stool collects, than at the upper end of the colon. The researchers also noted that the transit of food through the bowel was much slower in Britons than in Africans. Thus, constipation increases the risk of colon cancer. However, on further investigation, it became clear that other major differences also existed. There was a big difference in the amount of fat and sugar intake—both were very high in the British diet and very low in the Ugandan diet. The Ugandans did not eat animal fat, so their intake of saturated fat was lower. The researchers concluded that the saturated fat and sugar content, as well as the fibre content, were important.

We know that something stimulates the genes to change in the lining of some of the cells in the colon. Certain chemicals, radiation or just aging might stimulate this trigger gene. However, some speculate that this factor may be certain chemicals in fat and sugars and that fibre protects us by passing them through the colon more quickly. These chemicals may act either directly or indirectly by stimulating bile salts from the liver to produce a carcinogenic chemical. Researchers are now investigating the latest theory that this may be related to the number of oxygen-free radicals, which may alter the genes towards cancer. Until this is proven, however, it does seem prudent to follow a diet low in fat and sugar and high in fibre. The more fat and sugars and the less bran we eat, the higher the incidence of colon cancer and other diseases. An added benefit is that this is also a good diet to follow to prevent heart disease—the number one killer.

What Should We Eat?

Avoid fat, especially the saturated animal fat in beef, pork and lamb; substitute veal, fowl (without the skin) and fish. Enjoy lots of whole grain breads and cereals, fresh fruit and vegetables, to increase the amount of fibre in your diet, and don't forget that lots of water is required for fibre to work (see page 33). Eating fibre without drinking water is a total waste of time. Consider taking supplements of vitamins C and E and beta carotenes. These vitamins contain antioxidants, which prevent the oxidization that may be connected to cancer.

This diet should help decrease the carcinogenic chemicals affecting the genes and also the time they have contact with the lining of the colon.

Does Removing Polyps Prevent Cancer?

There is now plenty of evidence to prove the benefits of removing polyps in preventing colon cancer. The earliest study, done even before the colonoscope was invented, was *Gilbertson's Series*, in which rigid sigmoidoscopies were done every 2 to 3 years on a group of 18,150 subjects in Minnesota. All polyps were removed from the rectum at each visit. Dr. Gilbertson and his team found only 11 cancerous growths, some of these on the first visit. In three cases, the rectum was surgically removed because it was feared the cancer had spread, but not one subject had any residual cancer. This is because the cancer was found so early—the dangerous growths were small and localized.

The 11 cancers found represent 85% fewer cases of rectal cancer than among people who do not have regular rectal examinations. It is obvious that routine sigmoidoscopy with polypectomy significantly reduces cancer of the rectum.

In a study at the *Rudd Clinic*, colonoscopies were done on the executives of a major Canadian company over a period of 23 years.

During 700 examinations, 153 polyps were removed. In three people there were cancerous growths, which were removed; all were alive 5 years later. Others in whom the polyp could have become malignant were saved from getting cancer by having the risk removed.

The results of a polyp study carried out by *Dr. Sydney Winawer's* group at Memorial Sloan-Kettering Cancer Center, New York, were recently published in the *New England Journal of Medicine*. This study also supports our findings. According to these results, 90% of colon cancer can be prevented by doing regular colonoscopies and removing all polyps.

Prevention of Colon Cancer Compared with Other Cancers

Colon cancer is in a very favourable light when compared with other major cancers found inside the body, such as lung, breast, prostate and ovarian cancer. None of these can be diagnosed unless the cancer is already present. None of these can be prevented by removing a polyp-type pre-malignant lesion. Such cancers can only be treated and/or re-moved—not always successfully. Colon cancer is the only one with a polyp-like lesion that can be found before it starts to turn into can-cer—true prevention. Cancer of the cervix, not, technically, inside the body's cavity, is the only other type that can be prevented—ab-normal cells shown in a Pap smear may be pre-malignant. Removing the affected area by laser vaporization can stop cervical cancer from developing.

Finding a polyp in the colon and removing it, before it has turned into a cancer, results in a 100% prevention rate.

Mass Screening Programs for Colon Cancer

Surveying a huge number of people by testing a small piece of stool with a chemical for the presence of blood yields positive findings in fewer than 8% of those tested. These people must then have a colonoscopy to find the cause of the bleeding.

There are two types of tests used to screen for colon cancer: the hemoccult slide test and the ColoCARE kit. These tests are designed to detect a very small amount of blood in the stool—1 part in 5,000. However, there are problems with these mass tests—they are not specifically for cancer or polyps. Not all cancerous tumours bleed, and those that do only bleed sometimes and may not be bleeding on the test days. Polyps bleed even less frequently, and yet polyps are what we want to find most of all, because removing a polyp can prevent a cancerous growth from developing altogether. This lack of blood may result in a false negative test. The person tested may then have an inappropriate sense of security.

Another complication is that many other conditions are more frequent causes of bleeding than polyps and cancer: these include anusitis, piles, colitis, fissures, even bleeding gums and eating red meat before the test. These conditions would give a positive result and hence a false positive test. The person tested might then go through further examinations unnecessarily.

There are ways to increase the accuracy of these tests. Starting 3 days before and during the test, avoid red meat, horseradish, excessive vitamin C, ASA (Aspirin), laxatives containing mineral oil, and medications such as corticosteroids, reserpine, indomethacin and phenylbutozone. The tumour or polyp is more likely to bleed if there is extra roughage to scrape it as the stool passes, so increase your intake of foods such as popcorn, nuts, salads and other high-roughage foods.

One benefit of mass screening tests is that the general public becomes better educated on the subject of colon cancer. The emotional impact of hearing that cancer has been detected in someone as a result of such a program may also motivate others to participate.

The *hemoccult slide test* has been around for many years. Some doctors use it in their offices, but it lends itself rather better to large screening programs or surveys in the general population. It was used in Miami a few years ago by interested viewers of a television educational marathon on colon cancer. The test kit consists of a wooden stick and a special cardboard container with three sections. The wooden stick is used to pick up a little bit of the stool from the toilet and place it under the flip-top cover of the first section of the container. Another bit is taken from another part of the stool and placed in the other part of the same section. This is repeated on different days for sections two and three, and then the container is mailed to a laboratory.

The *ColoCARE kit*, a newer test, has the decided advantage, in that the stool does not need to be fished out of the toilet, placed on a card and sent away for further testing. It is a home test, clean and easy to do. The kit contains three test pads in a foil envelope and one piece of cardboard on which the results are recorded. On each test pad are two small squares and one large square, which change colour. For three separate bowel movements on different days, before toilet paper is used, one test pad is placed in the middle of the toilet water. After 30 seconds, the three squares are examined to see if any have turned blue/green. If so, the appropriate square is marked on the result card. The remaining pads are carefully replaced in the resealable foil envelope.

The test is based on the principle that blood tends to float to the surface of the water—where the test pad is. Reports suggest that this is at least as accurate as the hemoccult slide test in detecting blood, if not more so.

There is a slight disadvantage to this test from the doctor's point of view. Since these test cards are not sent in to a laboratory or doctor, there is no way of knowing who bought the test, who did it, or who had a positive or negative result, and there is no way to reach those whose results were positive to be sure they have a colonoscopy. This is a self-directed test—you have the privacy but also the responsibility to act if the results are positive.

My personal experience in organizing so many of these large screening programs is that colon cancer or polyps are often found not because of the bleeding that resulted in a positive slide test but because of the colonoscopy done for a positive test. So often the test is positive for other reasons, such as anusitis or inappropriate diet. The people tested are then examined by colonoscopy, and the polyp or cancer is found quite by accident. Nonetheless, these screening programs are effective in finding just under 3% of people with colon cancer; and they are cost-effective.

Current Research in Colon Cancer

Since we now know that six to ten different genes must be altered for colon cancer to develop, most current research is genetically oriented. The all-important trigger gene, which must change in order to start the whole process, is attracting a lot of attention. This gene was found defective in 1 out of 5,000 births; it is an inherited defect. These people get familial polyposis; most of them are dead from colon cancer in their 40s. The same gene was investigated in elderly people with colon polyps and cancers and was also found to be defective. In them, it was an acquired defect. This gives a great deal of support to the genetic theory.

The goal of this genetic research is to be able some day to detect the presence of this gene in cell scrapings from the rectum and predict which people are likely to develop cancer. Researchers hope to be able to correct this absent or abnormal gene by replacing it with a normal one or, possibly, by suppressing its triggering effect.

Other research is being done at other stages of the process. Some efforts are being directed at preventing the cell from duplicating and producing a polyp in the first place. Others are concentrating on the gene that allows the cancer to spread to another organ. Work is being done on stimulating the immune system so that it controls the duplication and spread of the abnormal cells and protects itself from damage by chemotherapy.

One Last Word

Once you've had a polyp, the chance of more polyps developing in the rest of the colon is three times greater than normal. Similarly, once you've had a cancerous growth, there is a 17% chance of developing a second one in a different part of the colon.

Yet most colon cancer can be prevented with routine colonoscopy and removal of polyps. In people who stick to the recommended follow-up routine, I rarely find colon cancer. When I do find cancer, it is usually in a patient I am seeing for the first time—it is very upsetting to everyone. These people may have never heard of colonoscopy, but I hope this book changes that.

Glossary

Abdomen—The part of the body located between the chest and the pelvis.

Anal Canal—The $1\frac{1}{4}$-inch-long (3 cm) channel that connects the rectum to the anal skin and is surrounded by sphincter muscles.

Anal Margin—The lowest end of the anal canal, where skin widens out into the buttocks.

Anoscope—A short hollow instrument with a light through which the doctor views the anal canal.

Anus—The opening of the anal canal.

Ascending colon—The part of the colon that extends from the cecum in the lower right side of the abdomen to the transverse colon in the right upper side of the abdomen under the rib cage.

Asymptomatic—Showing no symptoms.

Benign—Not malignant.

Cecum—The first part of the colon into which the small bowel empties and where the appendix is located, in the right lower abdomen.

Colitis—Inflamed lining of the colon.

Colon—The large intestine, which is 4 to 6 feet (1.5 to 2 m) long. Its function is to receive unabsorbed food from the small bowel and to absorb water to form stool.

Colonoscopy—Examination of the inner aspect of the colon with a special instrument.

Colorectal surgeon—Surgeon who specializes in diseases of the colon, rectum and anus.

Constipation—Fewer than one bowel movement a day with stool that is hard and dry or small and pebbly.

Cryoprobe—A metal probe used to apply cold to tissues.

Cryosurgery—The application of very cold temperatures to remove a lesion.

Cryotherapy—Therapeutic application of very cold temperatures.

Dentate line—The irregular line near the middle of the anal canal that marks the boundary between the mucosa and skin.

Descending colon—The part of the colon that extends from the transverse colon under the ribcage on the left side of the abdomen down to the sigmoid colon in the left lower abdomen.

Digital examination—Examination of the anal canal and lower rectum with the finger. Bidigital examination involves two fingers inserted into the rectum.

Dilatation—Stretching apart the anal canal to treat anal stenosis or widen a narrowed anal canal.

Diverticulitis—Inflammation or infection of one or more diverticula.

Diverticulosis—The condition of having diverticula.

Diverticulum (singular), **diverticula** (plural)—A pocket or pouch that starts in the lining and protrudes through the wall of the colon.

Edema—Excessive fluid (not blood) inside a tissue.

Enema—A procedure in which a liquid is introduced into the rectum for cleansing or therapeutic purposes.

Enzyme—Catalyst that speeds up a chemical reaction such as breaking down food.

Esophagus—The long tube that carries food from the mouth to the stomach.

Fecalith—A small, hard piece of stool.

Fibre—A chemical found in cereals, fruits, vegetables, nuts and seeds. Dietary or insoluble fibre is not absorbed into the bloodstream and adds bulk to stool. Soluble fibre is absorbed into the bloodstream and does not increase bulk in stool.

Fibrous tissue—Scar tissue made up of very strong fibres that do not stretch, usually the result of surgery.

Fissure (anal)—A tear or cut in the lining of the lower part of the anal canal.

Fistula (anal)—A false passage or tunnel between the anal canal and the adjacent skin.

Flatus—Passage of intestinal gas out of the anus.

Hematoma—A painful swelling near the anal margin, filled with blood clot.

Hemorrhoidectomy—Surgical removal of hemorrhoids, replaced by newer methods such as ligation and cryotherapy.

Hemorrhoids—see Piles.

Impaction (stool)—A large, dry, hard mass of stool big enough to block the rectum.

Infection—Invasion of the body by living microorganisms, often producing pus.

Inflammation—A protective response of the tissue to irritation or injury, usually indicated by redness, swelling and pain, which may become infected.

Intussusception—The slipping of one part of the bowel into the cavity of the part below.

Irritation—A reaction in the mucosa or skin, usually indicated by redness, pain and sometimes itchiness.

Lactose—A complex sugar contained in milk and milk products, beer and other foods.

Large bowel or intestine—see Colon.

Laxative—An agent that promotes evacuation by causing the bowel to cramp or irritating the lining. Not the same as stool softeners or bulking agents.

Ligation—Placing a tight elastic band around tissue (e.g., the neck of a pile).

Lumen—The inside cavity of a tubular organ (e.g., bowel).

Malignant—Cancerous.

Mesentery—An apron-like membrane that joins the bowel to the back of the abdominal wall and contains the blood vessels that flow to and from the bowel.

Mucosa—The inside lining of the intestinal tract.

Para-anal—In one part of the circumference of the anal margin.

Perianal—Around the entire circumference of the anal margin.

Peritonitis—Inflammation of the lining of the abdominal cavity, which may be caused by an infection.

Piles—Bulges of tissue attached to the upper end of the anal canal above the dentate line, containing blood vessels and covered by mucosa.

Polyp—A small, tumour-like growth shaped like a wart, cherry or cauliflower in the mucosa. Polyps in the rectum and colon sometimes turn into cancer.

Polypectomy—Removal of a polyp.

Proctologist—A surgeon who specializes in diseases of the rectum, anus and colon but does not perform abdominal surgery.

Prolapse—Protrusion. Prolapsed *piles* occur when the piles are big enough to protrude into the anal opening. Prolapsed *rectum* occurs when the lower bowel protrudes down through the bowel below and protrudes through the anus.

Rectocele—A bulge in the wall between the rectum and the vagina that protrudes into the vagina.

Rectum—The part of the bowel between the sigmoid colon and the anal canal.

Sigmoid colon—The part of the colon that extends from the descending colon to the rectum.

Sigmoidoscopy (rigid)—Examination of the rectum and lower sigmoid colon with a special instrument.

Signs—Evidence of a disease or condition that can be seen by someone else.

Skin tags—Excess bits of skin around the anal margin.

Small bowel or intestine—The 20-foot-long (6 m) bowel that connects the stomach to the colon.

Somatizer—A person whose anxiety or emotional problems cause physical complaints such as diarrhea.

Sphincter muscles—The two muscles that surround the anal canal. The internal sphincter muscle is normally contracted and prevents the passage of gas; the external sphincter muscle is a voluntary muscle that can be tightened at will to hold stool in the rectum.

Splenic flexure—The bend in the colon where the transverse and descending colons meet in the left upper abdomen.

Stenosis (anal)—The narrowing of the anal canal usually caused by a ring of scar tissue under the skin. The scar tissue encircles the anal canal so that it cannot stretch normally to allow for the passage of thick stool.

Stomach—The organ that receives chewed-up food from the esophagus, churns it up and passes it into the small bowel for absorption, located in the mid-upper abdomen. Often mistakenly used to denote the abdomen.

Stool—The waste product, made up of food residue, bacteria, intestinal secretions and decreasing amounts of water, that is formed in the colon and stored temporarily in the rectum.

Stool softener—Agent, such as fibre, that adds bulk to stool, thereby improving bowel habits and making stool softer and easier to pass.

Suppositories—A bullet- or tube-shaped capsule containing medication that is inserted past the anal canal and into the rectum, where it usually dissolves.

Symptomatic—Showing symptoms of a disease.

Symptoms—Evidence of a disease or condition as seen or felt by the individual.

Thrombosed piles—A (rare) blood clot in a pile. Inaccurately used to describe a hematoma.

Transverse colon—The part of the colon that extends from the ascending colon to the descending colon across the upper part of the abdomen.

Tumour—A swelling or enlargement caused by new, uncontrolled growth of tissue cells. It may be benign or malignant.

Index

Other health care titles available from Macmillan Canada:

The Foot Doctor
Revised and Updated
by Glen Copeland D.P.M., 1996
ISBN 0-7715-7370-7
A clear and concise self-help guide for a wide range of foot
    problems from one of Canada's leading podiatrists.

Pain: Learning to Live Without It
by Dr. David Corey, 1993
ISBN 0-7715-9199-3
Dr. David Corey offers a drug-free, step-by-step program for
    conquering chronic pain.

Taking Charge by Taking Care
by Marilyn Linton, 1996
ISBN 0-7715-7382-0
An overview of women's health care plus an indepth look at
    today's fifteen most important health issues from the lifestyle
    editor of the *Toronto Sun*.

Feel Fantastic
Maye Musk's Good Health Clinic
by Maye Musk, 1996
ISBN 0-7715-7384-7
A portable clinic that contains all you need to know to get started
    on a lifetime of health.